SCRANTON'S BYGONE DEPARTMENT STORES

SCRANTON'S BYGONE DEPARTMENT STORES

The Globe and the Dry

DANIEL J. PACKER JR.

Foreword by Keith Oppenheim

Published by The History Press
An imprint of Arcadia Publishing
Charleston, SC
www.historypress.com

First published 2025

Manufactured in the United States

ISBN 9781467159500
Hardcover ISBN 9781540299918

Library of Congress Control Number: 2025943934

Notice: The information in this book is true and complete to the best of our knowledge. It is offered without guarantee on the part of the author or The History Press. The author and The History Press disclaim all liability in connection with the use of this book.

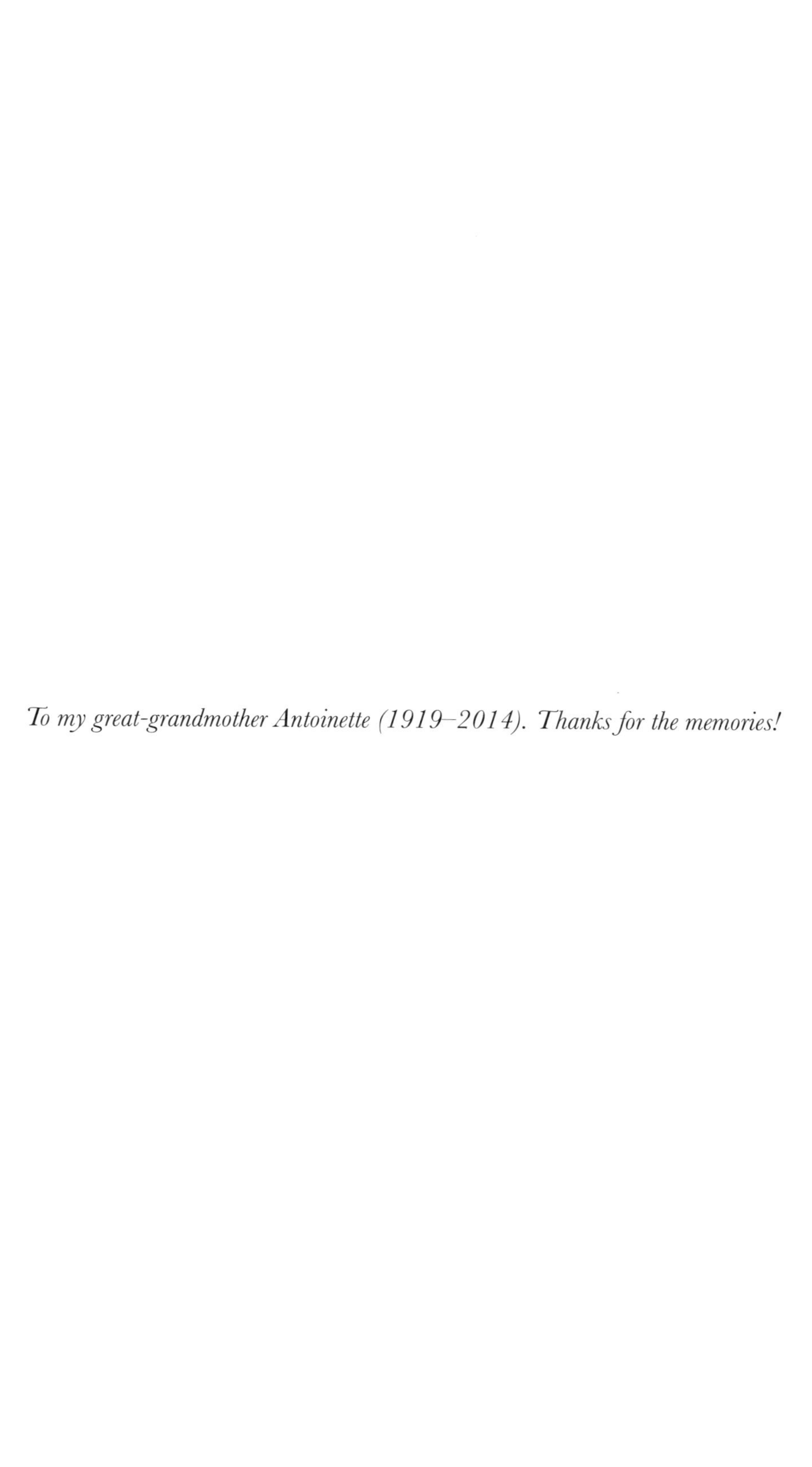

To my great-grandmother Antoinette (1919–2014). Thanks for the memories!

CONTENTS

FOREWORD

The Oppenheim's store of Scranton, Pennsylvania, is a miraculous story that began when our ancestors settled in (what was at the time) all four corners of the United States of America. They honed their merchant skills along the frontier lands of the Mississippi River until the opportunity to settle in Northeastern Pennsylvania years later allowed them to establish a department store that helped advance novel trends in the nation's retail landscape and catered to the needs of the wider community. This book takes the reader on a fascinating exploration of the history of department stores in America; the history of the city of Scranton, Pennsylvania; the community residing therein; and much more. I, along with the rest of the Oppenheim family, extend my great appreciation and thanks to Daniel Packer for undertaking this project. He reawakened in all of us, my immediate family and others, many memories, particularly of I.E. Oppenheim (a.k.a. Ike, the founder of the Scranton Dry Goods Company, later known as Oppenheim's) and of Scranton, as well as times spent with numerous other relatives (including, but not limited to, Uncle Ralph Mendel, who also worked in the store). Much of the research that went into this project produced information about known relatives who were also in the dry goods business, but moreover, it uncovered many new details concerning our family's connection to numerous other well-known retailers who have, since the 1800s, created a quintessentially American experience and enterprise.

In bringing the history of the Scranton Dry Goods Company (Oppenheim's) and its most well-known competitor, The Globe Store, to life, Daniel Packer reminds his readers of the golden age of department store retailing. His tale of how and why that age eventually succumbed to discounters and strip malls is as enticing as it is informative. While the Oppenheim family surely owes many thanks to Daniel Packer for this exceedingly rich undertaking, we also extend our gratitude to the many employees—those in the furniture, glove, lingerie and so many more departments, some of whom were with the store for sixty years or more—for their dedication, hard work, loyalty and, above all, community spirit. Of course, it also goes without saying that we add our great appreciation to the many customers of both stores whose enthusiasm for shopping sustained both businesses and their families.

The Oppenheim family first came to America from Germany when the store founder's grandmother died during childbirth, leaving her brother the task of looking after her first and only son. It was he, the child's uncle, who made the difficult decision to bring the infant to the New World, raising him as his own. Although life in America had much to offer them, tragedy struck again when that same son (Ike Oppenheim's father) eventually followed in his own mother's footsteps and died during early adulthood at the start of his own career, leaving behind Ike's mother and their young children. With divine assistance, as well as that of Ike's great-uncle (who brought the family to America and started their successful foray into the dry goods business), she carried on, finding the courage to establish and operate a retail business as a single mother in what was largely an outpost for traders along the relatively undeveloped frontier lands of the Wild West nestled between the northern head of the Mississippi River and Native American lands during the Civil War. The reputation of newly freed African Americans living and prospering alongside cowboys, Native American Indians, municipal townsmen and migrant traders passing through, all presented an enticing vision of a place where Jews could thrive alongside settlers of many backgrounds and walks of life. Although they were not entirely alone or unique in their pursuits, they were among the first of only a few who became merchants pursuing ethical values in addition to profits. Some of their relatives journeyed south as well, establishing retail businesses along the southern ends of the river, but none of them could have foretold how their perseverance would pay off for their offspring who later spread eastward toward more cosmopolitan (and increasingly more diverse) areas, going on to contribute to what became the dawn of the department store era.

While practicing their merchant skills, our ancestors joined together with other pioneering families at a time in American history when ethno-political strife tested social values. They became experts in the dry goods business but were as equally ambitious in their social lives as they were in their trade, pursuing civil justice where they found it. African American struggles for emancipation from slavery shaped their worldview, while the Civil War raged during westward expansionism. Subsequently, two world wars, predominantly centered within what was for many of the merchants their former European homelands, confirmed their commitment to conduct business in an ethical manner. With one another's help, that of their families and their wider American compatriots of many backgrounds, a small circle of Jewish immigrants envisioned a future and engineered a newly burgeoning industry to plan a life for themselves that, while being in some respects quintessentially American, also clearly reflected their own unique personal pasts and provincial dreams as well.

This was the context that introduced the Oppenheims to the fundamental nuts and bolts of the dry goods trade, but it also introduced them to a small cadre of other immigrant merchant families, some of whom went on to become the largest department store entrepreneurs in the nation. Whether due to family ties or fate, circumstance or faith, our ancestors drew together with these other similar merchants and, through the generations, went from settling along both ends of the Mississippi River in the 1800s to devoting even more hard work in the 1900s, establishing the Scranton Dry Goods Company. Names like the famed Maas brothers (of Florida); the Gimbels (who at one point presided over the largest department store conglomerate in the country); William H. Block (of the luxurious Block's store in Indianapolis); the Mendels, Kempners and Blasses (of Arkansas); and even the Burdines (of Miami, whose family was from the Aberdeen, Mississippi area long before they ever began retailing), as well as the Grumbachers of The Bon Ton Store chain, The Bailey's Company (of Cleveland) and others all helped advance American entrepreneurship with some of the most recognized department store brands of the nation. They also, however, all came from humble early American immigrant families who were intimately connected through blood, business, faith or circumstance to the Oppenheims and the path our family traversed over a century and a half of merchandising in the United States, which included the operation of a beloved institution in Scranton and the wider regional community. Maybe the most remarkable connection with other early American retailers, however, was the relationship that the Oppenheims developed with the Federmans (whose contributions to the industry gave rise to the Federmans' namesake stores, the Boston Store chain, as well as Interstate Stores Incorporated, which brought a great many brands to success, including Family Fair, Topps, White Front, Toys "R" Us and others).

Ellis Mendel Oppenheim Jr. (a grandson of the founders of the Scranton Dry Goods store) was the only third-generation Oppenheim to work in the store. Also known as Mr. O, he was actually the last in the generations to do so. I, his son, have been left the task of carrying on the legacy in other ways, but both of us are immensely pleased to see this book published. After digging deeply into family history, I discovered many previously unknown facts that are quite incredible. Perhaps the most astonishing thing that the author and I found was that there existed a deep relationship between the great-grandfather of Mr. O's beloved wife of fifty-three years, my mother, Lois Oppenheim, and Ellis's grandfather, the founder of the Scranton Dry Goods, Ike Oppenheim! When Ellis met Lois, she had never known anyone in retailing and was delighted to get to know the store as well as the Scranton area where they resided when first married, as her father had also grown up in the Wilkes-Barre/Scranton area, and thus it was a bit of a return home for her to live there temporarily. To learn decades later, however, that her great-grandfather on her mother's side had established the business in Scranton with Ike Oppenheim was an extraordinary surprise. It was all the more surprising given that her mother had been born in Lima, Ohio, and raised in Syracuse, New York, and there was seemingly no connection to Scranton, Pennsylvania, whatsoever. The best part, however, was yet to come, as the story proved not only that the two gentlemen were acquainted, as Lois and Ellis had previously been told, but also that they were in business together for a number of years and that they had launched together an enterprise that brought the Oppenheim family to Scranton in the first place over a century ago (and the Federman family to many other places throughout Ohio, New York, the Midwest and the rest of the nation).

Lois Oppenheim's great-grandfather was Marcus J. Federman (of the renowned Federman companies previously noted), but it was not until 2022 that Daniel Packer and I realized it was he, her great-grandfather who had first brought Ellis Jr.'s grandparents Isaac E. Oppenheim and Constance Mendel to Scranton in 1912 to run the store. This was only a few days after the birth of their son Ellis Sr., who, with his younger brother Richard, went on to succeed their father in the family business, which witnessed many years of local family purveyance. When Ellis Jr. and Lois Oppenheim first married and settled in New York City, Ellis worked at the Bonwit Teller store on Fifth Avenue. They have lived in New York City ever since, with Ellis working at various positions in wholesaling and retailing. The check for the purchase of the original building in Scranton has always hung inside Ellis Jr.'s home office, but it was not until the next generation that the pieces of the historical puzzle all started to fit together thanks to the research that went into the writing of this book. Daniel Packer, whose great-grandmother also assisted our family in Scranton over the years, initiated the daunting task of unraveling all the years of history that shaped the Oppenheim family's business endeavors in Scranton. It was then, with my undertaking more endless research and historical analysis, that we were able to recount the journey our family has taken over the generations across the American continent from European roots to the frontier lands, then on to New York and more recently beyond. A leather-bound book on how to treat customers written by Ike Oppenheim, along with various other memorabilia, is all that remains today of a history spanning more than 165 years of our family's contributions to American retailing.

The full story is truly an immeasurably intriguing read, and while it goes beyond the bounds of this one book, the author certainly presents herein a personally enriching and fascinating study. This book gives a worthwhile and enjoyable look into how the evolution of the retailing trade in America is more complex, intertwined as it is with relationships and developments in business practices, than is commonly known. There is much that will resonate with anyone who lays their hands and eyes on these pages, and much more that will be newly discovered by a great many other readers. It will inspire in all who delve into these pages the desire to continue to build on the American retailing tradition and learn about the history of what was much more than just a shopping experience. This book fosters a suspense from which the reader will be left asking when all the rest will be divulged and what in the future will be revealed about a profession that has its roots planted not only in the distribution of dry good necessities to the community around it but also in creating an experience where diverse families could partake in fashion, entertainment, socializing, eating and community-building that forged the bonds of society at large.

—Keith Oppenheim

PREFACE

Like a store directory, the preface serves to guide the reader through the various chapters and topics of this book. Inasmuch as The Globe and the Dry were similar in size, merchandise mix and general appearance, it is important to distinguish them from each other and detail the individual traits that made each so special. To this end, I have done my best to differentiate between them in each chapter. For many of the topics discussed, the writing proceeds just the way many Scrantonians describe their memories of shopping downtown—that is, start at The Globe and then go across the street to the Dry. Therefore, most of the chapters begin by discussing The Globe. Then, the reader will figuratively cross Wyoming Avenue to the Dry, where the history of that store will be explored. For other topics, both stores are discussed at the same time.

One instance of possible confusion is how one refers to the Dry throughout its sixty-eight-year history. While The Globe Store is almost always referred to by that name, the Dry is referred to by several variations of the store's formal title depending on the memories of the individual. As the store had a rather long name, "Scranton Dry Goods Company," many people affectionately shortened it to the "Dry," "Dry Goods," "Scranton Dry" or "Scranton Dry Goods." The company itself shortened the name in the early 1960s from "Scranton Dry Goods Co." to "Scranton Dry" in all print advertising and store packaging. This possible confusion over the name is further compounded by the fact that the company formally changed the store's name from "Scranton Dry Goods Company" to

"Oppenheim's" in 1972. For the sake of brevity and clarity, the store is referred to as the "Dry" for the majority of the book, with a few exceptions. When the writing reaches the point in the store's history when the name was formally changed, the store is referred to as "Oppenheim's." Hopefully, these touches provide consistency and clarity for the reader and enable them to relive an era of Scranton's history that is fondly remembered but will never be seen again.

ACKNOWLEDGEMENTS

When I was a young child with a peculiar fascination with department stores in general and The Globe and the Dry in particular, I could never have imagined the path my hobby would lead me down. It has been a journey filled with challenges, triumphs, fun and discovery. This project has helped me fulfill a long-held dream of writing a local history book, but I would have never been able to realize that dream without the help and encouragement of several family members and friends. First and foremost, I would like to thank my late great-grandmother as well as my grandmother and my mother for sharing their memories with me. They have truly inspired and guided me all my life. I would also like to thank the numerous friends who have helped and encouraged me along the way, some of whom I knew before this project and some I made because of it. This book would not have been written had it not been for the Oppenheim family's incredible help and generosity. I would like to extend my deepest and most heartfelt thanks to Mr. Ellis Oppenheim Jr.; Dr. Lois Oppenheim, PhD; Mr. Keith Oppenheim; Mrs. Susan Oppenheim Dimond; and Mrs. Ellen Oppenheim Feldman. It was my privilege to record the amazing history of their family business, and I so enjoyed the conversations I had with them.

I would also like to thank Mr. Greg Boock, who, along with sharing my interest in collecting local memorabilia, generously shared his and his late father's extensive photograph collection with me. Many of those photos appear in this book. Moreover, I would like to thank the late Mr. Robert J.

"Bob" Scheller Jr., who relentlessly encouraged me to pursue my study of local history and to share it with the community. My sincere appreciation to my friends and co-workers at the University of Scranton Weinberg Memorial Library who assisted in my research and offered invaluable advice and encouragement. The librarians at the New York State Library, Albany, also helped with my research, and for that I am sincerely grateful to them. Thank you to the many, many members of the Facebook page "Globe Store Scranton, PA" who generously shared their memories with me and provided valuable feedback when I posed questions to them.

Many thanks are due to the Lackawanna Historical Society (LHS) as well. As an undergrad at the University of Scranton, I volunteered at the LHS, where one of my duties was to help catalogue the extensive files of photographs and newspaper clippings in the library. I also had full access to its archives, which further fueled my love for the department stores discussed in these pages. I was elated when I found the newspaper images of the Dry's first floor in an old file marked "Scranton Dry Goods." I could barely contain my excitement as I ran over to the staff member on duty and asked for a copy that I still have to this day. The LHS staff were incredibly kind, and they never tired of my asking countless questions about The Globe and the Dry. I learned so much and made so many great memories during that time. Years later, when I embarked on this journey, I reached out to the LHS, where I encountered the same warm welcome and helpful attitude that made me feel so comfortable and confident as a young college student. For that, I extend my sincere appreciation and gratitude. Finally, I would like to acknowledge the many friends, co-workers and teachers who have encouraged me and helped me anywhere along the way. Many of them will probably never know what their simple acts of kindness or friendly attitudes mean to me, but to them I say a deeply heartfelt thank-you.

INTRODUCTION

I must admit one thing up front: I did not like shopping at The Globe when I was a child. At least I didn't think so at the time. When I thought of The Globe Store, I thought of endless aisles of clothing and shoes, the last things that I wanted to look at. When the holidays rolled around, I was filled with dread at the thought of having to make my annual trek to the store to see Santa Claus. While I appreciated the gifts I received from him on Christmas morning, the legendary gentleman himself greatly frightened me. After several escalator rides to the fourth floor, my terror grew as I ascended that final flight of steps known locally as the "Santa Stairs" to the fifth floor. There, in his magical "Santa's World," the jolly old elf in red was waiting for me as well as hundreds of other area children to hear what we wanted for Christmas. It was difficult to get me to smile for the obligatory photograph on Santa's knee. While the photographers were more successful some years than others, their attempts to ease my tension by shaking Bert and Ernie dolls in my face usually always had the opposite effect to the one that they desired. One picture shows me completely frozen in fear while another shows me wailing with tears streaming down my face. I do, however, have at least one picture that shows me at ease and smiling. This process was repeated each spring with the arrival of the Easter Bunny. His presence also unnerved me, but like Christmas presents, I appreciated the baskets filled with brightly colored eggs, small toys and goodies that he left on Easter morning.

While the service at The Globe was second to none, my six-year-old self did not appreciate it. Store associates would approach my mother, grandmother or great-grandmother in every department ready to assist with their every question, want and whim. This usually succeeded in making my journey through the forests of clothing racks and skyscrapers of shelving units even longer. One vivid memory I have of the service at The Globe is in the shoe department, where I was quite often as I was constantly outgrowing my footwear. There, The Globe employed a dapper gentleman who was dressed to the nines and had his hair combed so not one follicle was out of place. He assisted The Globe's guests in finding the perfect shoe, including its youngest customers. In that group, I was one of his more difficult clients. The Globe was one of the few stores at the time that still had staff members who personally assisted customers with finding and trying on shoes. Other area stores had discontinued this service in favor of the customer finding and trying shoes on their own, as well as using the foot measuring devices to find their size and that of their children. My family still preferred the former form of service, the old-fashioned model of the salesperson assisting the customer. Being a naturally shy child, I preferred the latter. I wanted my mother to take care of finding my shoes and measuring my feet. The Globe, however, was "our" store, and it was where nearly all my clothes and shoes came from. I can still remember the salesman taking the ice-cold steel shoe measuring device and pressing it to my foot. As he remembered who I was, he would say something along the lines of, "Your feet have grown again." He would then point to a colorful array of children's footwear for me to make my selection. I would choose something, and then, inevitably, my mother would choose something else. As she was paying, her opinion won out, and the dapper salesman swiftly retreated to a room behind a curtain to retrieve that shoe in my size. When he returned, he would put the shoe on my foot and check to see if it fit properly. As the old X-ray machines, or fluoroscopes, that were once used in stores to see how shoes fit were long discontinued for obvious safety reasons, the salesman would use his thumb to press into the front of the shoe to see where my toes were. Keeping in mind that my number-one goal at that moment was to leave, I would curl my toes to make sure that the shoe seemed like it was the perfect fit. He was wise to this and would ask me, politely but firmly, not to do that. After several attempts, this began to obviously frustrate him, as it did my mother, who was a bit firmer in her direction for me to uncurl my toes. Eventually, the salesman's polite persistence paid off, and I would finally leave with a brand-new pair of shoes. This is but one example of The Globe's courteous, professional sales staff. As a result of their efforts, I was a stylish '90s kid with the best sneakers, overalls and turtlenecks that the store could offer.

Looking back now, I have found that shopping at The Globe was actually one of the most enjoyable and memorable experiences I had as a child. I was thrilled with the store's unique architecture and quirky features such as the revolving doors, the Charl-Mont restaurant, the clanking, rumbling escalators the crisscrossed each other on each floor, the intricate medallions that were stamped into the circa 1908 tin ceilings and six floors of beautiful, ever-changing merchandise. I found the revolving doors particularly fascinating, as the opening sequence of a popular sitcom at the time, *Perfect Strangers*, features the main characters spinning round and round in one. I, of course, had to try that at The Globe, which I did to the other shoppers' delight (or annoyance).

At Christmastime, I loved the front of the store, as it glittered with twinkling lights, towering trees and shiny garland. Television commercials jubilantly announced the store's debut of its holiday décor, but nothing compared to seeing it in person. The Globe's display windows came alive with animated figures, dolls, stuffed animals, lights and fake snow. The displays could rival anything that larger stores in New York, Philadelphia and Chicago could conjure up, and they were a big treat to go see during the holidays. Even my fear of going to see Santa soon subsided as he calmly and gently coaxed me to sit on his knee and tell him what I wanted for Christmas. I'm told that, on one occasion when the store was not busy, he spent nearly half an hour talking to me before I felt comfortable enough to approach him. On another Christmas, the one special toy that I wanted more than anything was an electronic talking space shuttle that I had seen in a catalogue. I cut the picture out, and on this one occasion, I was actually eager to see Santa. When I think of this memory, it reminds me of another famous holiday story about a child who frantically climbed through a store-made winter wonderland to tell Santa about that one special toy he wanted for Christmas. I believe his was a Red Ryder BB Gun, but mine was no less special to me. Santa looked at the photograph I provided, and although The Globe did not carry it in its toy department, he promised me that he would do his best to get the toy for me. He put the picture in his pocket and sent me on my way. When the sun rose on Christmas morning that year, the toy space shuttle was sitting under the tree, just as Santa promised. Until age and maturity robbed me of my childhood belief in magic, I believed the real Santa Claus was at The Globe Store.

I also remember the toy department joyfully. At a very young age, this was where I received my very first toy that I got to select on my own: a Donald Duck doll. The saleslady was very kind and patient as she took down every stuffed animal that was on the shelf for me to examine carefully as I made my choice. It must have taken what seemed like forever, but she didn't mind. I was, after all, a valued Globe Store customer. It is memories like these that fill my heart with warmth and nostalgia.

The final memories I have of The Globe—the store's closing sales—are rather unpleasant. I remember walking across the newly constructed bridge from the Mall at Steamtown to The Globe's second floor. All the familiar sights and sounds were there: the tin ceilings, the shiny floors, the plush carpets, the constant rumble of the escalators and the high-pitched ringing of the elevator bells and manager call signals. The one thing missing was the merchandise. As I ascended to the fourth floor, I observed barren floors broken only by empty display tables, bare clothing racks, groups of naked and disassembled mannequins and a small smattering of leftover merchandise. When I got to the toy department, I was deeply saddened to find it empty. There was only one revolving rack left that had a few toys. I selected an old-fashioned tin top as my last purchase from The Globe Store. I saved it as a souvenir of my last trip, for, despite my young age, I had a strong sense that something very important was going away. It turned out to be the first of many items that I have collected from that store over the years. As The Globe passed away, it kindled my love of department stores and my drive to preserve their history while it is still in living memory.

I do not remember Oppenheim's Scranton Dry Goods Company, or the Dry, firsthand. Its life ended a few years before mine began. Despite this, my years of study and artifact collecting have given me a sense that it possessed all the same magical qualities that made The Globe so special. My great-grandmother told many stories of shopping there. She especially liked dining in the store's mezzanine tearoom, where one could observe the hustle and bustle on the first floor and wave to customers as they glided past on the nearby escalator. Many locals recall the giant Easter egg that was perched on the Wyoming Avenue entrance marquee that was just waiting to reveal Mr. and Mrs. Easter Bunny to a throng of excited youngsters screaming in delight. Still more will remember the escalators, which, prior to 1968, were wooden and are noted for the being the first of their kind in the city.

Facing each other on Wyoming Avenue, both stores engaged in a decades-long competition for Scranton's retail dollars that was fierce but friendly.

Downtown Scranton shoppers cross Wyoming Avenue from The Globe Store (*left*) to the Scranton Dry Goods Company (*right*). *From the Mark Boock Collection. Photo courtesy of Greg Boock.*

If The Globe was Scranton's answer to New York's Macy's Department Store, then the Dry was Gimbels. They complemented each other, and one is rarely mentioned without the other. In their efforts to be the best, they elevated retailing in Scranton to a level found only in larger metropolises and gave customers an unforgettable shopping experience.

Unfortunately, all they are now are memories. Scranton's great department stores are things of the past. At the time of this writing, the department store age is in its twilight. The sun set long ago on many revered retail names such as John Wanamaker, Marshall Field's, Gimbels, Hudson's, Kaufmann's, Filene's, B. Altman, Lord & Taylor, Abraham & Straus, Hess's, Horne's, Burdines, Pomeroy's and The Bon-Ton. The few that have managed to survive have lost much of their cachet through overexpansion, mergers, loss of regional identity and increasing competition from discounters and online retailers.

One of The Globe's famous slogans was "a gift from The Globe means more." That, in retrospect, was very true. Inasmuch as it has been decades since anyone has shopped at either store, one can now realize that The Globe and the Dry were more than just places to buy a new dress or a toy train. Both stores were the economic and cultural centers of the area. They were beacons of service, charity and community spirit. They helped us mark and celebrate our milestones. They were there when one needed a baptismal gown, first communion outfit, a suit for a Bar Mitzvah, a prom dress and a gift for a birthday or religious celebration. The professional sales staff was there to set a young man's mind at ease as he nervously selected an engagement ring for his potential bride. They also were sure to make a blushing bride-to-be shine in a wedding dress that would eventually be passed down through the generations. Finally, and perhaps most importantly, the stores provided a place where one could dream of the future and the promise that it held.

Many say that nothing lasts forever. What does last forever, if properly preserved, are memories. Hopefully, the memories in these pages will live on in the minds and hearts of those who walked those sales floors and be passed down to those too young to remember when downtown Scranton was a thriving hub of activity and the beating heart of Northeastern Pennsylvania.

I

SETTING SALE FOR NEW WATERS

Most of America's great retailing institutions had humble beginnings. Many started out as one-room shops while others began with nothing more than a peddler's cart and a dream. The stories of The Globe and the Dry are no exception. Both had modest origins and, through hard work, dedication and good business sense, managed to become some of the largest and most respected mercantile institutions in the Northeast.

In the late nineteenth and early twentieth centuries, the Industrial Revolution caused a great shift in where most American families lived and worked. Hordes of people flocked to the young nation's cities, attracted by the promise of steady work in factories and mills. Consequently, downtown business districts across the country enjoyed unprecedented crowds of customers anxious to purchase the wide array of wares being sold in the many shops that lined the streets.

In Scranton, it was a most fortuitous time to found such a business. Formerly known as a mostly agrarian area called Slocum Hollow, Scranton was first incorporated as a borough of Luzerne County in 1856 and later as a city in 1866. The nascent city was the product of the merger of three boroughs: Scranton, Hyde Park and Providence. By 1878, it was the industrial center of the newly organized Lackawanna County.[1] The thriving iron industry, which had been cultivated in the region by brothers George W. and Selden T. Scranton and their associates when they founded Scranton, Grant & Company in 1840, first cemented the burgeoning municipality's status as an economic powerhouse. Evolving into the Lackawanna Iron and Coal Company, the Scranton brothers' firm was an industry leader in iron production. So successful was the company with its production of the "T-rail," controlling interest in a railroad was purchased to transport its product to its major customer, the Erie Railroad, as well as to areas in New York and the Midwest. The Lackawanna and Western (L&W) Railroad became the Delaware, Lackawanna and Western Railroad (DL&W) when it was merged with the Delaware and Cobb's Gap Railroad in 1853 and became a major employer for the city's residents. Soon, the Scranton brothers' firm began producing steel before it moved its operations to Lackawanna, New York, at the turn of the century.

As lucrative as iron and steel were initially, it was Scranton's abundance of the fuel that drove the Industrial Revolution that held the most promise for the young city: coal. More specifically, the region's subterrain was rich in the highly sought-after variant known as anthracite coal, which burned longer, cleaner and more efficiently than the more plentiful bituminous, or soft, coal.[2] By the early 1900s, coal had supplanted iron and steel as Scranton's major industry. The city became the anthracite capital of the world, and the wild success of "King Coal" helped foster the growth of other powerful industries in Scranton such as garments, textiles and an ever-expanding network of railroads. The Scranton Lace Company was one of the largest examples of the many companies and factories that provided stable blue-collar jobs for the city's people.

Flush with jobs and investment opportunities, Scranton attracted newly arrived immigrants seeking a better life. They came from Ireland, Wales, England and Germany and later from countries in central, eastern and southern Europe, including Poland, Hungary, Ukraine, Lithuania, Russia and Italy.[3] The city's population surged. The census of 1900 showed that the city's population had doubled in twenty years. It was in that year that Scranton's population surpassed 100,000, making it the thirty-seventh-largest city in America.[4] Rising in population and prominence, Scranton could be a tough town to please as the vaudeville acts that frequently played there soon found out. "If you can play Scranton, you can play anywhere" became a popular phrase entertainers used when referring to the city's sometimes merciless theater audiences. As the first urban center in the nation to operate an electric streetcar on November 30, 1886, Scranton became affectionately known as the "Electric City."[5] At night, the downtown glittered like a clear sky full of stars with flashing, brightly lit signs that heralded everything from a fancy-dress shop to a regal theater to a grand hotel. The conditions were ripe for its two budding department stores to put down strong roots and grow into great retailers.

The Great White Way. The lights shined brightly in the Electric City when night fell. Here the many storefronts with their electric signs illuminate Lackawanna Avenue in the early twentieth century. *Author's collection.*

Other stores came and went in Scranton, but none proved to have the size, scope and staying power that The Globe or the Dry would eventually develop. One of the most notable examples was Clarke Brothers, which was an innovative retailer that dealt in dry goods and groceries. The company enjoyed great success in the early twentieth century and grew into a chain of stores throughout Northeastern Pennsylvania. Unfortunately, due to several factors, it did not enjoy the longevity that The Globe and Scranton Dry had. By the close of 1926, Clarke Brothers was gone.

The First Trip Around the Globe

The Globe Store's journey to prosperity is as remarkable as it is complicated. Its roots can be traced back to January 7, 1852. On that date, John Simpson was born in Stonehaven, Scotland, to Alexander and Margaret (née Logan) Simpson.[6] At the tender age of fourteen, Simpson became an apprentice to a dry goods dealer.[7] It was here that he cut his teeth in the retailing profession. Evidently, Simpson found that he had a knack for salesmanship and marketing as he chose to make it his lifelong career.

After three years as an apprentice, the then seventeen-year-old Simpson immigrated to the United States of America.[8] His career as a merchant soon began to flourish in this new land. He first settled in Rochester, New York, where he landed a job at the prestigious Sibley, Lindsay and Curr Department Store, or Sibley's, as it was affectionately known. After only eight months at Sibley's, Simpson left upstate New York in search of his fortune in Northeastern Pennsylvania. Soon after arriving in the city of Scranton, Simpson landed a job as a clerk at the retail firm of Lindsay & Liddle, also known as the "Boston Store," on Lackawanna Avenue in the city's bustling downtown. Simpson could not have known that taking this job would not only change his professional life but also set in motion a chain of events that would greatly affect Scranton's economy for generations to come.

In 1873, John Simpson joined forces with the man who was to be his business partner in what would become his most successful mercantile venture.[9] John Cleland, like John Simpson, was of Scottish ancestry.[10] He was born in Wishaw, Scotland, in 1849, and his father was a merchant.[11] He was introduced to business at a young age, first "serving his apprenticeship as a draper in the Hamilton stores at Glasgow."[12] At twenty-three, Cleland set his sights on the promise of unlimited business opportunity in the United States. With his parents' blessing, Cleland came to America and settled in Scranton, where he found work with Lindsay & Liddle.[13] Here, Cleland met and befriended his colleague John Simpson.[14] Cleland and Simpson remained with the Boston Store until 1873, when they joined forces and set out on their own.[15]

The newly formed partnership of John Cleland and John Simpson saw opportunity in the nearby village of Danville in Montour County. It was in that budding city that they founded their first store in 1873.[16] It soon grew to be the most prosperous retail establishment in town. After three years, despite their meteoric success as proprietors of their own store, John Simpson left Cleland in charge of the operation while he returned to his previous employers as a partner in Lindsay & Liddle of Scranton.[17] After a brief time, Simpson reteamed with Cleland and they continued building their company. The ambitious young men soon planned on expanding their increasingly successful firm to other towns. They set their eyes on Pittston, where they founded their second store in 1877.[18] Like the Danville store, the Pittston operation was a success from the opening day. Cleland and Simpson rode the wave of their newfound success while

Portraits of all The Globe's presidents beginning with the store's founders, John Cleland and John Simpson. *Author's collection.*

simultaneously improving their craft with their two thriving stores.[19] Later, they sold their stores in Danville and Pittston to focus on their flagship store in the growing city of Scranton.[20] Having both worked as merchants in that city, the two men had firsthand knowledge of the wildly prosperous future that seemed assured in Scranton thanks to the coal and mineral-rich soil below and thriving industry above. Scranton was fast becoming the center of commerce, culture and industry in an area that was helping build and power the nation. Scranton, at the time, had the potential to become a world-class metropolis. A most fitting location for a store called "The Globe."

In 1878, Cleland and Simpson settled on a location on Wyoming Avenue in the city's central business district to open their new "Globe Warehouse."[21] Initially, the store's full name was "Cleland-Simpson Company—Globe Warehouse." It was common practice at the time to give stores long names to delineate their owners and their sophistication. Stores across the country were given names that added a touch of class such as Boston Store. Boston was the center of imports and high fashion in that era. In addition to Scranton's Boston Store, other cities, including Wilkes-Barre and Erie, Pennsylvania, Utica and Binghamton, New York, and Milwaukee, Wisconsin, all boasted their own Boston Stores. Other fancy store monikers included New York Store, Bon-Ton, Bon-Marché and the Globe. The Globe name gave Cleland and Simpson's new business a continental flair and a promise of quality merchandise from around the world. Despite its worldly name, the store's initial sales space was relatively modest. A small room on the first floor of the Library Building served as the selling area for the new business.[22] In its totality, the first store had

The Globe's first home in the Library Building on Wyoming Avenue. *Author's collection.*

a mere fifty-foot frontage facing Wyoming Avenue with a depth of one hundred feet.[23] The Library Building was constructed by Horace B. Phelps in 1870.[24] It served as the Scranton Public Library until a new library was erected by John J. Albright at Vine Street and North Washington Avenue in June 1893. After Phelps's death, the building was sold to Elias Morris.[25] Eventually, Morris sold the structure to the Cleland-Simpson Company, which subsequently renovated and enlarged the building to accommodate their growing retail business.[26]

The Cleland-Simpson Company grew again when a third partner was added, William Taylor.[27] William's brothers David E. and John Taylor also joined the growing business in 1877 and 1886, respectively. According to Lackawanna Historical Society Director Mary Ann Moran-Savakinus, D.E. Taylor had been an employee of Cleland and Simpson.[28] Together, the Brothers Taylor showed great talent and promise. As such, Cleland and Simpson welcomed the Taylors as equals and gave D.E. control of their newly founded branch store in Allentown, Pennsylvania.[29] It was William's brother John, however, who was instrumental in running and expanding the Allentown branch and thus made the Queen City his home. Around this time, the company's first and only out-of-state branch was established in Trenton, New Jersey. Eventually, these branches were sold or closed. The partners' expansion plans going forward focused on Northeastern Pennsylvania, which was manifest in their new store in nearby Carbondale.[30] This branch was later sold as well.[31] Unlike the Allentown and Trenton stores, however, the Carbondale operation continued as a going concern long after its disassociation from the company headquarters in Scranton. Despite these setbacks, Cleland, Simpson, & Taylor, as it was now known, was enjoying tremendous prosperity in Scranton and Pittston. It became clear, however, that the company's future lay in Scranton, not Pittston. Therefore, the Pittston operation was shed on July 10, 1896, along with its general manager, Charles K. Trumbower, who was listed as a partner in the business at the time.[32] Full control of the Pittston store was then transferred to Trumbower. John Taylor also officially dissolved his partnership with Cleland and Simpson on that date. He then assumed full ownership and control of the Allentown store. John continued to build on its success and even founded a branch in nearby Bethlehem before selling both locations to partners Edgar E. Knerr, Harvey H. Knerr and R.M. Rauch in April 1919. While he is mentioned in the 1896 Notice of Dissolution, D.E. Taylor remained with the company for a few more years before he ultimately dissolved his partnership and sold his interests back to Cleland and Simpson on June 6, 1901.[33] Although he is not mentioned in either the 1896 or 1901 Notices of Dissolution, it is probable that William Taylor left the company around this time as well. Now a duo once again, John Cleland and John Simpson chose to focus all their time, energy and ingenuity on their Scranton store.

In the mid- to late nineteenth century, the concept of a "department store" was foreign to most shoppers. A new and revolutionary model of retailing, the department store offered customers an unprecedented array of merchandise under one roof. Prior to this new era, stores generally dealt in one or two lines of goods. As such, shoppers had to visit several different shops to purchase all the products they wished to acquire. For example, a woman looking to purchase a new outfit would have to visit a dressmaker, a millinery shop, a glove shop and a shoe store in order to complete it. Department stores consolidated these small stores and allowed customers the convenience of making all their purchases in a one-stop shop. Additionally, department stores introduced the concept of browsing—that is, leisurely perusing the products on the shelf without being pressured by sales staff to purchase anything. The small shops, by their nature, were not conducive to browsing as most of the merchandise was kept behind the counter. The store clerk oversaw the selection of merchandise for the customer to examine. Intended or not, there was always an unspoken expectation that the customer would make a purchase and hence a certain pressure was placed on him to do just that. Department stores, in contrast, placed the merchandise on the sales floor on open shelves and racks allowing shoppers to touch and examine the wares at their own pace. Shopping itself suddenly became a form of entertainment. It also became a social activity where one could meet family and friends for a day of browsing and conversation. Thus, department stores radically changed the way Americans viewed the act of buying goods.

SPECIAL
BARGAINS
RECEIVED DAILY
—AT THE—
GLOBE WAREHOUSE,
711 HAMILTON ST.,
ALLENTOWN, PA.
SCRANTON,
PITTSTON,
CARBONDALE, PA.,
TRENTON, N. J.
CLELAND, SIMPSON & TAYLOR.
March 28—ly1

An advertisement listing the various store locations owned by Cleland, Simpson & Taylor. *Author's collection.*

As proprietors of one of the first large department stores in the city, Cleland and Simpson were innovators when it came to changing the shopping habits of Scrantonians. That was immediately evident in their adoption of a fixed or one-price policy. That is, all the merchandise in the store would be sold at the price as marked on the sales tag.[34] No bartering would be permitted. Previously, most merchants employed a policy where the listed price was simply a starting point from which the customer and the salesperson would haggle until an acceptable amount was reached for both parties. Pioneered by Philadelphia merchant John Wanamaker and the Straus family of New York's Macy's Department Store, fixed pricing quickly became the accepted norm in retail. When The Globe advertised goods at a certain price, it was understood that that was the price the customer would pay. For example, a February 15, 1913 advertisement for the Globe Warehouse enticed locals to browse sale items such as gowns "from the plainest to the most elaborate; at from 45c to $8.50." Other items included $2.25 satin bedspreads, a pair of Irish Point Curtains for $3.25 and, a Special Saturday only, $1.00 men's shirts on sale for $0.76.[35] This new pricing strategy streamlined the sales process, improved customer service and increased profitability.

Another new concept in retail at the time was the advent of ready-to-wear clothing. The Globe and stores like it across the nation were founded during a period when less than half of all clothing, or soft lines, were made ready-to-wear.[36] Many customers, particularly women, purchased fabric, laces, patterns and trim to make their own clothes. According to John Beck in his *Never Before in History: The Story of Scranton*, clothing manufacturers had learned to mass-produce clothing due to the high demand for military uniforms during the Civil War.[37] Innovative and new, department stores provided the perfect setting to market ready-to-wear clothing to eager shoppers.

After the departure of William Taylor from the company, the business was incorporated as the Cleland-Simpson Company with John Simpson serving as president. On January 5, 1912, John Cleland, one-half of the brainchild that founded and perfected The Globe, died suddenly after suffering his second stroke in his city home at 520 Madison Avenue.[38] Left without his friend and partner, John Simpson was forced to carry on the business alone. He purchased his late partner's interests in the company and continued at the helm, helping steer The Globe toward becoming one of the largest and finest department stores in Scranton. Despite his immeasurable contributions and legacy, it would be Simpson's descendants who would continue in his footsteps and build the store into a retailing powerhouse that dominated the landscape in Northeast Pennsylvania for generations.

The Dry Gets Its Feet Wet

Like The Globe's origin story, the Dry's is one that is both fascinating and complicated. The Dry's story began decades before the store's founding in 1912 and far beyond the city limits of Scranton. It began in Mississippi, where on July 6, 1881, Isaac E. Oppenheim was born in Aberdeen to Emanuel and Regina Oppenheim.[39] Emanuel Oppenheim worked as a confectioner in that city. Soon after, the family moved to Vincennes, Indiana, where Emanuel had relatives in the shoe and dry goods business. Emanuel worked as a manager in the family stores until poor health forced his departure. In March 1885, Emanuel Oppenheim died of kidney disease at the age of thirty-five, leaving Regina with six young children to support on her own. A woman of strength and ingenuity, Regina soon found a way to support herself and her family when she opened her own millinery shop specializing in women's and children's hats.[40] As soon as her children came of age, they all entered the retail profession in one form or another to help support their household. In addition to working in the family business, the Oppenheims became friendly with another aspiring retail family, the Gimbels, who also started out in Vincennes.[41] The Gimbels would go on to revolutionize department store retailing and become part of American popular culture with stores in several major American cities, a legendary rivalry with Macy's on New York City's busy Herald Square and a role in the holiday classic *Miracle on 34th Street.*

I.E., or "Ike" as he was affectionately known, began honing his craft as a merchant while he was still a young man.[42] His experiences at various retail firms throughout the Midwest taught Ike valuable sales and customer service skills.[43] During his family's time in Vincennes, Ike took a position as a clerk at the retail firm of I. Joseph and Sons.[44] In 1898, he left that company to accept a job at the famed William H. Block store in downtown Indianapolis. While at Block's, the young Oppenheim was exposed to many of the methods and traditions that were part of the operation of a large department store. This education would serve him well later in his career. For a few years prior to 1911, Ike Oppenheim was working as a traveling linen salesman for Henry Glass and Company of New York City. His friend and colleague, Jacob Hiram Vineberg, was a fellow traveling salesman who sold tinware for the Indiana Tinware Company. Finding that they had much in common personally and professionally, the two men had formed a friendship and at one point struck up a conversation where they talked about the hardships of life on the road.[45] Both disliked the constant travel, time away from family, poor hotel accommodations and less than appetizing meals that they were forced to endure as part of the job.[46] They agreed that if a store could be found that had a promising future and was within their price range, the two men would pool their savings, purchase it and leave their life on the road behind.[47] To this end, Oppenheim and Vineberg became business partners. During his travels, Oppenheim happened upon an excellent business opportunity while in Akron.[48] There, the Akron Dry Goods Company, a department store organized and run by businessman Marcus J. Federman, was for sale. Legend has it that while stopping in the Akron Dry Goods to sell the store linens, Oppenheim received an offer to buy the business in return. Marcus J. Federman was a well-known operator of dry goods establishments and department stores throughout the East Coast and the Midwest. His company, which by 1928 became known as Interstate Department Stores, operated large retail outlets in several major cities, including Akron, Ohio; Lansing and Flint, Michigan; Paducah, Kentucky; and Scranton, Pennsylvania. By 1927, the Federman group of stores controlled twenty-three stores across several states.[49] It showed a net profit that year of nearly $1 million and was hugely successful.[50] It should be noted that, despite newspaper articles implying the sale began with a chance encounter, it is highly probable that Ike Oppenheim and J.H. Vineberg were well-acquainted with the Federmans as friends and fellow businessmen as early as the 1903. Additionally, as Ike had made his home in the Akron area by 1910, it is possible that he was at least familiar with the Akron Dry Goods, if not previously involved with its operation in some capacity.

A youthful portrait of I.E. Oppenheim in 1917. *From* The Tribune, *July 18, 1917, page 21.*

Not wasting any time, the fortunate Oppenheim immediately sent a wire to his partner and told him of the offer.[51] It seemed the opportunity of a lifetime had fallen into their laps. The two men communicated back and forth throughout the night via telegraph, running up twenty-four dollars in fees, not an insignificant amount of money in those days.[52] By that morning, the two men had agreed to purchase the Akron Dry Goods Company from Marcus J. Federman.[53]

Finally able to bid adieu to their lives on the road for good, the two ambitious young men immediately set out to expand and improve the Akron Dry Goods Company into one of the city's finest department stores. Starting with twenty-five thousand square feet of floor space spread over three floors, the store eventually expanded to forty-five thousand square feet of space spread across two buildings that were connected by an arcade.[54] The retail complex rose six stories high at its apex; one could walk into the main entrance on busy Main Street and walk an entire city block before reaching the rear exit on neighboring Howard Street.[55] The expanded store could accommodate fifty departments covering a wide range of merchandise for Akron customers to peruse.[56] Oppenheim and Vineberg also set out to build a first-class buying, management and sales staff. To this end, they thoroughly organized and expanded the size of the staff in all departments. In addition, they maintained buying offices in their home city of Akron as well as New York City in order to keep abreast of the latest trends.[57] The New York buying office was part of a buying unit that was associated with 143 stores across the country.[58] Thus, in a few short years, the two men had transformed the Akron Dry Goods Company from a mediocre mercantile establishment into a premier department store in one of Ohio's largest cities.

After Marcus J. Federman sold the Akron Dry Goods Company to Ike Oppenheim and J.H. Vineberg, he continued to build his retail empire. He returned to Akron several years and numerous expansion projects later to grow another large store alongside his brother Leo G. Federman. Federman's at Mill and Main Streets boasted far more floor space than his family's previous Akron stores and represented their most ambitious attempt to make a lasting mark on the retail landscape of that city. It succeeded a previous incarnation of Federman's on South Howard Street that had been founded in 1904 by Marcus's brothers, Benjamin, Leo and Charles. It also followed several earlier locations, including one in Youngstown, Ohio, but those stores were smaller and did not last. The five-story Federman's store was in operation until its closure in 1958.

An advertisement for the Akron Dry Goods Company's "Vineberg Day" sales event. The store's five-story building in downtown Akron, Ohio, is depicted in an artistic rendering. J.H. Vineberg is pictured in the lower right corner. *From the* Akron Beacon Journal*, May 9, 1934, page 7. Author's collection.*

In addition to Akron, Marcus J. Federman set his sights on other cities in Ohio as well as those in neighboring states. One of them was the prosperous city of Scranton. Rich with natural resources, industry and labor, it was the perfect place for the expansion of his company. To achieve this goal, he searched for and found a relatively small space at 111–13 North Washington Avenue in the city's downtown.[59] The building, which had been formerly occupied by another retail establishment, J.D. Williams & Brothers Company, was owned by another duo of ambitious merchant princes, Samuel and Benjamin Samter. The Brothers Samter owned and operated a large men's and boy's clothing store, Samter Brothers, on the corner of Lackawanna and Penn Avenues. By the 1910s, it had become one of the city's premier purveyors of fashions for the family.

With a location and plan in place, Federman declared to the *Scranton Truth* that he intended "to give Scranton a metropolitan department store in every particular. This field offers big opportunities for it is a city that has a great future."[60] He vowed that his store would undersell any other in the city and that the merchandise carried would be of superior or equal quality to that carried elsewhere in the city. Federman had big plans for the store. He initially planned to make Scranton his home base and operate his company and raise his family from the growing city. He hired local architect Edward Langley, who also designed The Globe Store's new building on Wyoming Avenue, to develop plans for erecting additional sales floors on top of the structure, and he began negotiations to purchase a large building nearby to serve as a warehouse.[61] Many of these auspicious plans did not come to fruition for Federman, but fortunately for the city and for the Oppenheim family, the Scranton Dry Goods Company did.

At eight o'clock on March 9, 1912, the new Scranton Dry Goods Company formally opened to great fanfare at 111–13 North Washington Avenue.[62] The atmosphere surrounding the event was festive to say the least. The front of the store was festooned with banners and swags of red, white and blue, and virtually the entire inventory was placed on sale.[63] What the event lacked in flowers and souvenirs, it more than made up for in bargains for shoppers and an army of one hundred clerks standing at the ready to cater to their customers' every whim.[64] Federman and the staff had worked tirelessly for weeks to prepare the store for opening by creating attractive and exciting displays as well as making certain that every surface was spic and span.[65] The store's first two 51-by-175-foot floors were devoted entirely to the display and sale of wares.[66] The third floor was devoted to stockrooms and the wholesale department.[67] Throughout the store, customers could find a wide range of dry goods, including bedding, linens, petticoats, dresses, children's clothing, raincoats, suits, silks, notions, rugs, millinery and curtains. As Federman and his team intended, the crowds that jammed the sales floor

The New Kind of Store

SCRANTON DRY GOODS CO.

111-113 N. Washington Ave.

Merchandise

The new store will handle mechandise that the public may absolutely depend upon.

Merchandise for everybody's requirements, and so priced as to be within the reach of all, and always value for the price asked.

The public will find everything at the Scranton Dry Goods Co. that is dependable and desirable.

Remember that the Scranton Dry Goods Co.'s prices for good merchandise will be lower than anywhere else.

There are many reasons for this, the greatest of which are Talent, Ready Money and Experience.

Our general buyer, Mr. Federman, has been working hand in hand with the manfacturers, so that the Scranton Dry Goods Co. may give the people values hitherto unheard of.

Watch for the Opening Date!

A 1912 Scranton Dry Goods Company advertisement promoting the new store's attributes. *Author's collection.*

The new Scranton Dry Goods Company prepares to open in March 1912 as passersby try to get a glimpse of the exiting wares within. *From* The Scranton Truth, *March 8, 1912, page 5.*

on that first day were awed by the store. The Scranton Dry Goods Company was a success. Federman seemed destined to build the Scranton store into his greatest achievement to date. Fate, however, would intervene, and like he did with the Akron Dry Goods Company a few years earlier, he chose to pass that opportunity on to someone else.

The someone else Marcus J. Federman chose as his successor in Scranton was none other than his young protégé from Akron, Ike Oppenheim. Federman had given Oppenheim and his business partner, J.H. Vineberg, their first real opportunity to build their own business in the burgeoning department store industry. Now he was going to give Oppenheim the opportunity to build a store on his own.

Initially serving as the general manager and chief officer of the Scranton Dry Goods Company, Oppenheim moved to Scranton with his growing family, which had come to include a wife, the former Constance Mendel of Hot Springs, Arkansas. The Oppenheim and Mendel families had known one another for generations, which is most likely how Constance and Ike met. The Mendels of Hot Springs were, like the Oppenheims, also in the retail trade, owning and operating several stores in their community. The couple wed in Hot Springs on December 28, 1909.[68] Constance and Ike initially settled into a comfortable home on Dodge Avenue in Akron. Shortly before moving to Scranton, Constance gave birth to the couple's first son, Ellis Mendel, on March 8, 1912. Ellis was followed by a younger brother, Richard, in 1915 after the Oppenheims had moved to Scranton. Upon moving to Scranton, the family set up a homestead first on Monroe Avenue and then on Myrtle Avenue in the city's prestigious Hill Section. Ike later purchased a large country estate in nearby LaPlume called Hilcrest. Hilcrest featured picturesque grounds, a lake and gardens that supplied flowers and plants for the store's garden center. Eventually, Hilcrest became the Oppenheim family's primary residence. With a growing family and an esteemed position at a flourishing retail business, the ever-enterprising Oppenheim had created a future abundant in opportunity and promise for both him and the city he now called home.

2
ESCALATING SUCCESS

From humble beginnings to phenomenal success, The Globe and the Dry grew tremendously during their early years in terms of sales and of size. Their quick rise from one-room shops into multi-floor palaces of retail is a testament to the hard work, perseverance and innate talent of their founders.

The Globe: Reaching New Horizons

At the turn of the twentieth century, The Globe—or the Globe Warehouse as it was then called—still occupied the old Library Building on Wyoming Avenue. A major fire on March 27, 1889, had heavily damaged the structure and destroyed most of the inventory.[69] The company suffered estimated losses of $169,000 in stock, $23,000 in damages to the building and $4,000 in the loss of furniture and fixtures.[70] Despite this enormous setback, Cleland, Simpson and Taylor, who was still with the company at this point, quickly rebuilt. Although the business now took up the entire structure, which was enlarged and renovated after the fire, the store was still in great need of additional sales and stock space. More departments were being added, and the current building could not be expanded any further. The solution was to build an entirely new structure designed and built especially for the Cleland-Simpson Company.

Around 1904, the Simpsons commissioned noted local architect Edward S. Langley to design the new store building. The result was a handsome, impressive five-story structure with a basement. The design was modeled in the Chicago School style of architecture with neoclassical details, which was prominent in retail design during that period. In 1906, the new store was completed. Its façade featured clean horizontal and vertical lines complemented by several intricate details. These details included pilasters with ionic capitals, floral bas-reliefs and a central fan window located on the fourth floor. The ground floor featured large floor-to-ceiling display windows capable of displaying the newest wares and fashions. The windows guided customers to the main entrance in the center. Like icing on a cake, the entire structure was crowned with a beautiful green cornice above a band of relief letters that proudly read "1878 Cleland Simpson Company 1906." This, of course, was the year the store was founded, the formal name of the business and the year of the current building's completion. The new store's completion date was also proclaimed in Roman numerals in the central block of the cornice railing. In response to the disaster that had devastated the business in March 1889, the new building also included a modern fire suppression system. Sprinklers lined the ceilings of every floor, and the building was topped with a large water tower that quickly became a landmark in the city. When the store formally premiered its new house, Scrantonians were amazed by its beauty, size and many modern features. In just eighteen short years, The Globe had grown from a one-

The need for more room has been pressing hard for many months but it will not be very long until we have

A NEW GLOBE STORE

for you, larger, better and more convenient for you. This is the store that was "Built for Scranton" and Scranton simply demands more, as this store produces about everything called for, it also produces a bigger and better store when the shopping public asks for it by their increased response and buying needs—that is the sort of store you want. While the building goes on business suffers no interruption.

An advertisement touting the benefits offered by The Globe's new building. *Author's collection.*

room shop into a palatial five-story department store in which Scranton took great pride. The new store became a symbol of the city's economic prowess and cultural sophistication.

Around the time the new store was completed, the owners decided to drop the "warehouse" moniker in favor of a simpler and more sophisticated-sounding name: The Globe. It should be noted that during this early period of growth, the company experimented on the order of the name. In the beginning, the name Cleland and Simpson, or Cleland, Simpson and Taylor, was always placed above the Globe name. The logo often appeared at the top and the bottom of newspaper advertising. As the years passed, the naming strategy was gradually reversed as customers began to refer to the store as simply "The Globe" or the "Globe Store." Eventually, management decided to drop the Cleland-Simpson Company name entirely in print advertising and the store's packaging.

By 1917, even the new building could not contain the rapidly growing business. To accommodate it, the two six-story buildings on the right side of The Globe were acquired from the Scranton Supply and Machinery Company. Interior walls were broken down and the floors were renovated so that the décor was harmonious from one building to the next. Shallow ramps and steps were constructed where floor levels differed so customer traffic would be unobstructed throughout the store. Edward Langley was reemployed by the firm to lead the redesign of the new addition. Edwin S. Williams, a local contractor, was tasked in carrying out Langley's vision for the store while having the added challenge of not disrupting the business day or disturbing customers.[71] Other firms such as Wolf & Wenzel and Schillinger Brothers were hired to carry out more practical projects such as plumbing and tile work.[72] In one of the restrooms alone, more than eight thousand ceramic tiles were required to cover the walls.[73] An equal or greater number of rubber tiles were used to cover the floors of the entrance vestibules.[74] To attach them, nine thousand pounds of Portland cement was used along with two thousand pounds of hydrated lime and twenty-five thousand pounds of sand.[75] The exterior of the store received no less attention. Langley's design called for the existing façades of the acquired structures to be removed and replaced with one that matched the original store. The recessed sixth floor, while not spoiling the exterior look of the building, created additional space for stockrooms and offices. During the project, business was not interrupted for even a day. Newly expanded and renovated, the Globe Store formally premiered its new look to Scranton in September 1917. As in 1906, the space wowed customers and drew interest from residents and the local media alike. An article published in the *Scranton Republican* on September 13, 1917, stated that "truly shopping is no longer a task to be dreaded but one of the happy events of this twentieth century when one finds the styles, qualities, merchandise and needfuls [*sic*], with all the ease, comforts and conveniences that are to be found in this modern store home."[76]

The exterior renovations gave The Globe a unified, if uneven, façade. This issue was rectified a few years later in 1923 when property on the left side of the store was purchased and the existing buildings were demolished. This time, Langley designed an entirely new structure that matched the original store exactly, both inside and out. By the mid-1930s, The Globe had a frontage spanning 150 feet on Wyoming Avenue and included five full

The Globe's first expansion to its five-story store. Note the slight difference in color between the original and new façades. *Courtesy of the Lackawanna Historical Society.*

floors, one partial sixth floor and a basement. The structure was undoubtedly impressive for a retail establishment in a small city. Additional renovations took place in 1937 and 1939 that saw the ground floor and second floor of fashion completely redecorated. In 1940, air-conditioning was installed. This proved popular with customers anxious for a respite from scorching summer weather, so the store installed additional units in 1947. A 1953 advertisement for the store proudly proclaimed, "Today, the Globe Store is really 35.8 Miles Long."[77] It went on to say the following:

> *If The Globe were divided into separate buildings, each department the size of a small store, and lined up along one street front, you could walk miles and miles and miles past The Globe as you did your shopping. But instead of hiking these many miles you can have just as much to choose from, just as many stores to visit, all in one trip on The Globe's escalators and elevators. Under the big roof at The Globe is a shopping city of dozens and dozens of separate stores, each a small shop in itself, catering to the needs of its particular clientele. Each shop is individually managed to give more personal attention to those of certain sizes, shapes, ages, tastes, and budgets. Find your special shops here at The Globe and you'll enjoy the luxury of shopping with people who are specialists in your every want and need... know, too, that besides these, we have countless other departments that work for you "behind the scenes," setting the stage to make your shopping easier. Yes, The Globe is Scranton's largest store.*[78]

With its new, wide frontage, The Globe was able to provide an expansive, unbroken line of display windows at street level. In an era when shoppers used public transportation such as trolleys or simply walked to get around the city, "window shopping" became a favorite pastime of many. Passersby often stopped to gaze at the latest fashions or newest gadgets and toys that the stores had to offer. Hence, a store's windows became its calling card. The better and more attractive the windows, the more likely it was that potential customers would be drawn through the doors. The Globe's visual merchandising team took full advantage of this and lavishly spent time and money to create elaborate window displays to lure shoppers.

The massive building also enabled the Simpsons to add more varieties of merchandise than ever before, as well as many modern conveniences. New departments included a full restaurant, a beauty salon, a bargain basement, furniture, candy, bakery, major appliances, sporting goods and toys. Toyland, as it was called, always featured the latest and most popular

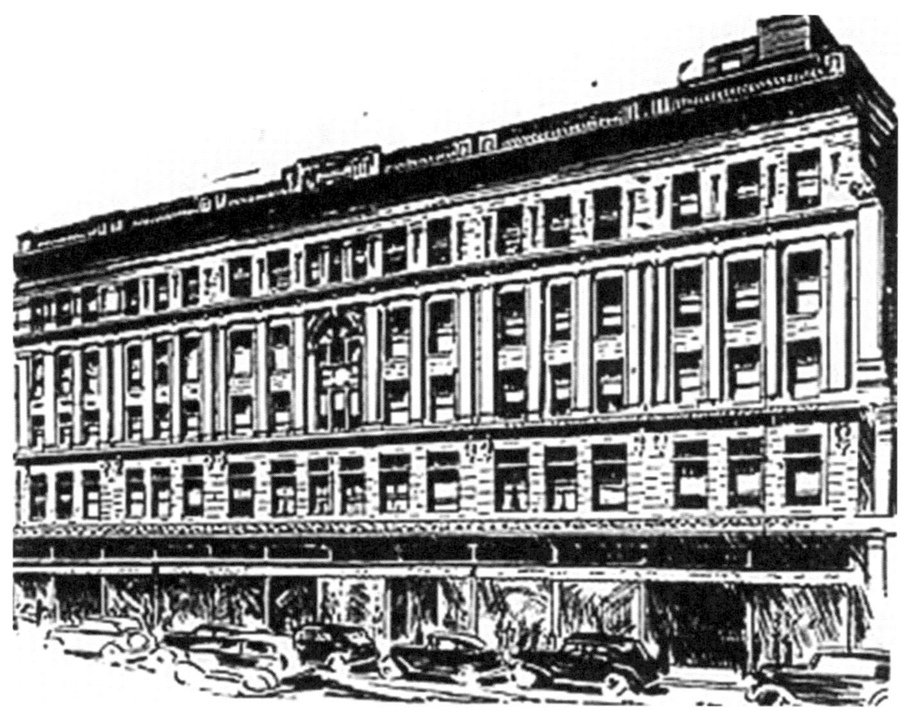

An artistic rendering of The Globe Store after the 1923 expansion from a company advertisement. *From a Globe ad, Author's collection.*

toys for boys and girls. Old standbys like dolls, trains, teddy bears, tea sets, bicycles and board games were always on hand. The store's buyers, however, were also sure to include the new "in" toys of the day. In 1953, for example, the western genre was extremely popular in entertainment and merchandising. Roy Rogers, a television cowboy hero to many children, was particularly well-liked, especially among young boys. The Globe's toy buyers responded by purchasing Roy Rogers outfits to display on the sales floor. They came complete with a brown felt cowboy hat, a washable shirt, a western tie with metal slide loop, a black western belt with raised pearl cross gun handle, Roy Rogers's double gun and holster set and western-style pants. Though each item was sold separately, a young cowboy could look just like his idol for $11.44, a relatively substantial amount for a toy in 1953. Lower priced items were also offered to please The Globe's youngest customers such as a play doctor set for $2.95 or a Dutch girl doll for $1.98. Thus, The Globe offered a toy for every taste and every budget. Inasmuch as management teams would place toys in the farthest locations they could find, The Globe's Toyland switched floors several times, often moving from the third to the fourth and/or fifth floors depending on the season. Having Toyland on an upper floor was advantageous to the store. Management could count on pesky children hounding their parents to visit the toy department, thereby forcing them to walk through all the other departments that they had not planned on visiting. Management hoped that these treks to Toyland would spur parents to make one or more unplanned purchases as they passed through the merchandise.

Toys were only one of the many offerings that the Globe contained within its four walls. Another was a complete book department with a lending library on the street floor. This department carried both the latest, most popular titles as well as the classics. Customers could purchase books new or used copies at discounted prices. Depending on the customer's wishes, they could buy the book at the retail price or borrow it for just three cents a day. The store did charge a bit more to borrow some nonfiction books at five cents a day, but few customers complained about the price. First installed on the second floor in 1926 as the Womrath Library, The Globe's lending library proved to be a popular service with customers until it was phased out in the 1950s.

In addition to books, The Globe maintained a complete music and records department on the street floor. Carrying the latest albums by the most popular artists, this department was very popular, particularly among young people. One notable publicity stunt for this section occurred in 1951 when popular tenor and actor Mario Lanza made an appearance at the store. The young singer was mobbed by overly excited fans who, in their zeal to show their affection for him, ripped his coat and shirt from his body.

Shopping for an entire day could be tiring for many customers. To give shoppers, particularly women, a respite, The Globe's new building provided a large ladies' lounge on the second floor. Here, female shoppers could adjust their appearance, socialize with other customers or simply relax on comfortable furniture. For those who patronized the lounge, many remember an aspect of shopping that is not allowed in stores today: smoking. Until the late 1980s, it was not uncommon for stores to allow customers to freely use tobacco products while shopping. As a result, the room was almost always filled with a thick cloud of tobacco smoke.

To navigate this massive, multi-floored emporium, a sophisticated vertical transportation system was installed. Eventually, The Globe had four passenger elevators, two on either side of the store, to whisk customers to every floor. Initially, the elevators featured immaculately uniformed operators who would call out the merchandise on the customers' chosen floors as they traveled. Later, the elevators were modernized to be self-service.

For those customers who were leery of using an elevator, the store offered staircases from the basement to the sixth floor. This, however, was inconvenient for those who had a lot of packages and bags to carry. The store would need another option to transport customers who were fearful of elevators. The solution to this problem came in 1947 when The Globe installed escalator service between the first and second floors. Additional escalators were installed in 1948 that extended the service to the fourth floor. Built by the Otis Elevator Company, these automatic stairs crisscrossed each other in the center of each floor and made traversing The Globe a much more convenient experience. The store advertised the new service, which happened to coincide with the store's seventieth anniversary celebration, by stating, "To serve you better, we open our new Otis escalators—all the way up and all the way down."[79]

As it was never used as a regular retail floor, The Globe's fifth level was not made accessible by escalator, but it could be reached by either elevator or by an elaborate staircase located in the rear of the fourth floor. The fifth floor was used primarily as an annex during peak shopping periods when additional sales space was required. This was particularly evident during the holiday shopping season, when the floor would often become the home to Santa's World. The fifth floor also featured the store's Community Room. The Community Room was an auditorium that could host special events for the store and the community such as fashion shows, cooking demonstrations and home-decorating presentations. It was also occasionally lent out for charitable causes as part of the store's continuing dedication to bettering the community. Most of this floor, as well as the sixth floor above, was given over to stock space, the medical infirmary and the employee cafeteria and break rooms. The top floors also created space for comfortable executive offices and boardrooms. It was here that John Simpson and his successors kept their offices and, like a captain on the bridge of a great ocean liner, helmed the huge store, steering it through good times and bad.

Arguably, the most troubled waters that The Globe weathered were those known as the Great Depression. As the world economy tumbled on October 24, 1929, a day known as "Black Thursday," and fell to depths not known before in the history of the industrialized world, department stores across the nation faced oblivion as hordes of customers suddenly became unemployed and unable to purchase merchandise. The Globe successfully weathered the storm of the Great Depression thanks to the hard work of its staff and the ingenuity of its leadership, but not without major heartbreak along the way.

On December 14, 1936, The Globe suffered a major setback when store president John Simpson passed away in his home at 308 Clay Avenue. He had served as the company's leader and an important figurehead in the city for over sixty years. His loss was immeasurable to both. Gone was the man who had shaped and guided The Globe from its beginnings as a humble one-room shop in 1878 to a palatial six-story department store at the time of this death. His was a long shadow and filling his shoes would be incredibly difficult, but The Globe would need a new captain, a new leader, to steer it out of the economic slump that was gripping the city and

Bargain hunters anxiously crowd in front of The Globe waiting for the doors to be unlocked. *Courtesy of the Lackawanna Historical Society.*

An artistic rending of The Globe's updated Wyoming Avenue façade and Men's Store Annex in the adjacent Hotel Jermyn. *Author's collection.*

the country. The man who succeeded John Simpson was his son-in-law Dr. J. Urbane Noble. Dr. Noble served for only a decade, but he did manage to leave his mark on the store during his relatively short tenure. Noble, like Simpson before him, was willing to make major changes and take risks in order to build on the success the store had already achieved and continue to meet the ever-changing customers' demands. It was he who guided the store as America faced another world war, making it an active participant in the local war effort. He also opened the store's appliance center and warehouse on nearby Linden Street in the 1940s, which enabled The Globe to expand its offerings of major appliances and to store stock off-site. This freed up space in the main store for more sales space and additional departments. A forward-thinking merchant, he also oversaw several major remodeling projects in the late 1930s that, as previously mentioned, saw the renovation of all the retail floors, the installation of escalators and the addition of air-conditioning.

After Dr. Noble died on October 10, 1946, the founder's grandson John R. Simpson took the reins as store president. He would remain in that position until 1949, when he was named president of the Third National Bank and Trust Company in Scranton. Despite his only serving a few years, one of John R. Simpson's most significant contributions was the addition of the men's store on Wyoming Avenue in 1948.[80] Spilling over into the Omar Room on the street floor of the adjacent Hotel Jermyn, The Globe's Men's Store offered area gentlemen formalwear, neckwear, sportswear, hats, umbrellas, accessories, watches and other forms of men's jewelry.[81] Designed by the prestigious firm of Amos Parrish & Company, well-known department store consultants at the time, the new space promised to be one of the most complete and modern of its kind in the area.[82] One of the more unusual additions to the Men's Store was the

A 1958 advertisement for The Globe's expanded main floor and Charl-Mont Restaurant. *From the* Scrantonian Tribune, *May 4, 1958, pages 34 and 35.*

R TODAY'S LIVING
CIALLY FOR YOU...
e beautiful, First floor!
RESTAURANT
SODA FOUNTAIN
Symbol of the Confidence
nton's Bright Future...
1 roof. Visit our new Charl-
sparkling new and large depart-
Globe ...
Visit Our New
Auto Centre, 138 Penn Ave.
.ESPECIALLY FOR YOU!
New! STATIONERY DEPT.
The Globe Store's New Main Floor
New! HAT BAR
The Globe Store's New Main Floor
New! CHARL-MONT RESTAURANT
The Globe Store's New Main Floor
New! BAKERY SHOP
The Globe Store's New Main Floor
New! SPORTSWEAR DEPT.
The Globe Store's New Main Floor
New! CAMERA DEPT.
The Globe Store's New Main Floor
New! MAJOR APPLIANCE DEPT.
The Globe Store's New Main Floor
New! LIBRARY DEPT.
The Globe Store's New Main Floor
New! HOUSEWARES DEPT.
The Globe Store's New Main Floor
New! NOTIONS DEPT.
The Globe Store's New Main Floor

Stag Shop in 1953. Intended to prevent the embarrassment some men experienced when walking into the women's departments to purchase a gift for a wife or significant other, the Stag Shop was placed in a discreet corner of the men's department and carried various and sometimes intimate gifts for women, including lingerie, nylons and expensive perfumes. Perhaps most important to The Globe's often hesitant male customers was the department's separate entrance on Wyoming Avenue. This saved them from having to trudge through the rest of the store and was an added convenience for those looking to make a quick purchase. The new men's store also offered "Dublecheck [*sic*] Fitting Service" to its male clientele—alterations for no charge.[83] Additionally, the department boasted that it would carry "163 sizes and models to fit almost every man."[84] By building the men's store in this manner, The Globe demonstrated that the customer was always first and foremost in the thought process of any expansion or improvement project.

Following the departure of John R. Simpson, another one of the founder's grandsons, John A. Noble, became president of The Globe. Following in the footsteps of his predecessors, Noble instituted major changes in

The Budget Shoe Department located in The Globe's basement in 1969. *Author's collection.*

THE YOUNG MEN'S SHOP

The Globe's new "Young Men's Shop" in the Men's Store Annex was one of the many departments in which local gentlemen could peruse the latest fashions for all ages. *Author's collection.*

merchandising. One of his major accomplishments was his making The Globe a member of Frederick Atkins Inc.—a department store buying cooperative based in New York. He also began a major expansion and renovation program in 1956 that would make The Globe Scranton's largest store and one of the state's finest retailers. Also like his predecessors, Noble became a beacon of citizenship and a community leader. When he made his home in the Scranton suburb of Clarks Summit, the street on which he lived was most aptly named. At the time of this writing, that roadway still bears the name Noble Road.

Despite losing its founding fathers and enduring many national crises, including a worldwide economic meltdown and two world wars, The Globe continued an upward trend and achieved new heights of success thanks to the dedication and talent of John Simpson's descendants.

The Dry: Moving On Up

Shortly after its opening on March 9, 1912, the new Scranton Dry Goods Company wasted no time in establishing itself as one of the city's most ambitious and value-conscious retail firms. With the backing of department store magnate Marcus J. Federman and under the watchful eye of store manager I.E. Oppenheim, the store took Scranton by storm. Just as in Akron a few years prior, Federman changed his plans and decided not to make Scranton his home base. A bout of ill health had forced Federman to reconsider his plans, and he offered his young protégé yet another opportunity of a lifetime when he offered Oppenheim the chance to make the Scranton Dry Goods Company his own store. Oppenheim agreed and purchased the company outright from Federman. Initially labeled as a branch of the Akron Dry Goods Company, Oppenheim continued his business association with his partner, J.H. Vineberg, and they operated both stores as one company. This arrangement lasted until the late 1920s, when Vineberg formally bought Oppenheim out of the Akron Dry Goods Company on November 27, 1927.[85] Scranton Dry Goods, however, had discontinued advertising itself as a mere branch of the Akron Dry Goods some years before. Under Ike Oppenheim's direction, the Scranton Dry Goods Company, or the "Dry" as many locals affectionately referred to it, was positioning itself as Scranton's second premier department store.

After a successful opening season and purchasing the Dry from Federman, Ike Oppenheim did not rest on his laurels. He quickly began a program of expansion in terms of merchandise and the physical space that his store occupied. Oppenheim's daughter-in-law Jane Oppenheim stated in 1992 that "the business was a full department store from the very beginning."[86] A few months after the store's grand opening celebrations, Oppenheim purchased the stock and fixtures and annexed the facilities of the nearby Taylor-Browning Company and John G. McConnell stores.[87] The McConnell Store, rebuilt following a devastating fire, faced Lackawanna Avenue and was the perfect location for expansion of the Dry. The two buildings were connected, giving the Oppenheim's business a direct entrance to Scranton's main business thoroughfare.[88] Oppenheim had learned the value of having multiple entrances on different streets in Akron as that store also faced two busy streets. He was sure to emulate that success in Scranton. Throughout the store's infancy, Oppenheim became known as a man who didn't mind taking big risks and making brilliant business deals. He acted quickly when the stock of other stores became available and purchased them to add to his growing emporium. Examples of this quick-minded business sense are further manifest in Oppenheim's purchases of the entire stock and fixtures of the T.E. Green, Mittleman and Kaufman and Goldsmith's Bazaar stores. The Goldsmith's acquisition is of particular interest, as Oppenheim made that deal within a few days of the store's closing and only an hour after inspection. Shortly after, he held a huge sale of its merchandise in the Dry.[89] To build confidence and loyalty in his customers, Oppenheim created a motto for the store that would also serve as its guiding philosophy and a solemn promise to its customers. The motto simply said, "Sincerity in purpose, honesty in dealings, and loyalty to truth."[90] There was no doubt by this time that Oppenheim and the Dry were successes in Scranton. They had both become institutions in the city, and Oppenheim's business savvy was proving to be the Dry's winning ticket.

No stranger to hard work, Oppenheim would often work "collarless and coatless" alongside his employees late into the night stocking merchandise or assisting his associates. The *Scranton Times* described him in 1916 as a "man of action" and "a young man who combines the aggressive business type with that of sound and conservative judgement."[91] Oppenheim's style was such that he earned praise from employees, customers and the local media alike as they publicly dubbed him Scranton's "merchant prince."[92] Furthermore, his employees thought of him as a "prince of employers" who led by example—that is, he believed in setting the pace for the organization by working hard himself instead of using a hands-off or authoritarian management style. He was therefore actively involved in every facet of his store's operation from customer service to accounting to maintenance and everything in between. He knew every employee personally and was always available to lend an ear to them for any of their concerns. If someone needed a job, Oppenheim would make every effort to find a place for him or her in his store. He also firmly believed in justly compensating his employees for their hard work.

In return for his fair and kind treatment, he had the loyalty and dedication of his associates. Turnover was extremely low at the Dry. Some of his employees would go on to serve the company for decades into the future. His customers also exhibited an undying loyalty to Mr. Oppenheim and the Scranton Dry Goods Company thanks in no small part to his treatment of them as guests in his store. Perhaps the greatest example of Oppenheim's kindness and generosity was exhibited during the Great Depression. Knowing his employees were hurting, he would often anonymously purchase coal to heat his associates' homes and have it delivered to their houses. He also looked out for his customers in the same fashion. After the Dry closed in November 1980, a former employee waxed nostalgic when remembering that she once witnessed Ike Oppenheim's pathos and largesse toward store patrons firsthand. She stated that during the height of the Great Depression, a young pregnant woman walked up to the candy counter on the street floor and ate a piece of candy without paying for it.[93] The salesclerk tending the counter then walked toward her and confronted the young woman.[94] Oppenheim, who was descending on the escalator, observed the commotion nearby and quickly intervened.[95] After being told by the woman that she had several young children at home to feed and that she had little food for herself, he took a bag and filled it with candy.[96] He then gave it to the young woman free of charge and said that in her condition and circumstance she had nothing to fear.[97] He then instructed the salesclerk not to approach another pregnant woman who ate a piece of candy without paying again.[98] With that, he said, "A piece of candy taken under these circumstances will never break me and the Scranton Dry Goods Store."[99] Ike Oppenheim's leadership style and down-to-earth personality endeared him to almost all who worked and traded with him.

By 1916, the Scranton Dry Goods Company had grown to include multiple buildings that faced both North Washington and Lackawanna Avenues in the middle of the city's busy downtown. In just a few short years, however, the Dry had again outgrown its current location. As such, Ike Oppenheim would need a structure large enough to accommodate his ever-growing business, monumental enough to position it as a worthy competitor to the city's other grand department store, The Globe, and close enough to the store's current building to maintain its prime location as an anchor in the central business district. He found it a few doors down at one of downtown Scranton's most prestigious addresses. Standing at the corner of Lackawanna and Wyoming Avenues, a department store of grand proportions and great beauty had been built to match the finest stores in larger cities. Rising four stories into the air, the structure was a vision of the neoclassical style with many intricate details and architectural flourishes. Built at a time when electric lighting was in its infancy, it featured large floor-to-ceiling windows on all levels to let in natural light as well as a central atrium incorporated for the same purpose. It was the perfect match for Oppenheim's growing store and ambitions. There was just one problem: it was already occupied.

The Jonas Long's Sons department store had conducted business in the building since its grand opening on December 10, 1897. Before then, the site hosted the Wyoming House Hotel, which opened in 1852.[100] The once grand hostelry had been Scranton's finest until its closure in 1896. That

A group photo of Jonas Long's Sons employees in front of the downtown Scranton store on October 21, 1898. *Author's collection.*

year, the old Wyoming House was demolished by the executors of the estate of noted local judge, businessman and philanthropist John Handley.[101] Handley's estate and its executors owned the Wyoming House and the land underneath it. To replace the hotel, plans were made for a new, ultramodern structure capable of accommodating the large Jonas Long's Sons store. The financial backing for the project was provided by the Judge Handley estate, and prominent architect Lansing C. Holden of New York was commissioned to design it.[102]

Completed in 1897, the new building was considered the finest of its kind in the city. Its new tenant, Jonas Long's Sons Dry Goods Company, already had a long history of doing business in Northeastern Pennsylvania. Founded in 1860 by Colonel Jonas Long, the company's first location was on Wilkes-Barre's Public Square. That store was housed in a handsome Victorian structure that rose five stories and was crowned with three enormous triangular adornments. Architecturally, the Wilkes-Barre store had a unique shape thanks to its location on one of the corners of the square. This also allowed for the building's centerpiece: a monumental three-story arch that framed the store's main entrance. Proud of the monumental building that housed its numerous departments, the company billed itself as the "Big Store" in local newspaper advertisements. With the new building at Lackawanna and Wyoming Avenues, the store's owners hoped to repeat their success in Scranton with an emporium of equal size and grandeur. The Scranton store did not disappoint, and Jonas Long's Sons quickly signed a twenty-year lease with the Handley estate. To compensate for their prime central city location, the company agreed to pay $25,000 a year in rent.[103]

All went well for Jonas Long's Sons until 1916, when the store's lease with the Handley estate expired.[104] From that point on, Jonas Long's began operating under short six-month leases.[105] The executors of the Handley estate had begun quietly disposing of the properties owned by the trust, and Ike Oppenheim, seeking a new, larger location for the Scranton Dry Goods Company, saw opportunity and acted decisively. In a deal that made headline news, Oppenheim figuratively bet the company and purchased the Jonas Long's Sons building from the Handley estate in August 1916 for $600,000, an astronomical sum for that time.[106] An article published in the *Scranton Times* on August 8, 1916, stated that the deal was "one of the quickest put through real estate circles in many years" and that "only a few days of negotiations were carried on before a substantial payment was made binding the sale."[107] The enormous risk factor was not lost on the local media or local business leaders. If Oppenheim was wrong, his company would quickly founder. Making a binding payment of $350,000, Oppenheim effectively shut out other bidders, including executives from Jonas Long's Sons and a banking firm that hoped to turn at least part of the building into one of their locations.[108] The "sons" of Jonas Long's Sons issued a quick response. Colonel Arthur Long, stung by defeat, defiantly announced to the local press that there would be no change in the company's operations in Scranton.[109] His company's lease did not run out until April 1917, and he was fully confident that his firm could find an equally suitable location in the city's downtown.[110] It wasn't to be. After vacating its location at Lackawanna and Wyoming Avenues, the store never reopened in Scranton. It never even finished out its current lease, which ironically gave the Dry's archrival across the street a chance to finish out Long's lease and occupy the building while its store was undergoing substantial remodeling and expansion.[111] The Cleland-Simpson Company had purchased the remaining stock of Jonas Long's Sons and held large sales of the surplus merchandise.[112] During this period, the Cleland-Simpson Company conducted business on both sides of Wyoming Avenue. Thus, it can be said that the building most associated with the Dry was The Globe for a very short time before Ike Oppenheim could formally assume ownership.

As for Jonas Long's Sons, its Wilkes-Barre store began to falter as well. On February 1, 1917, Jonas Long's Sons sold their Wilkes-Barre outlet to William F. MacWilliam. MacWilliam had risen through the ranks at the competing Fowler, Dick and Walker—The Boston Store on South Main

Street, and he was eager to run his own store. A mere decade later, the failing MacWilliam's store was sold to Pomeroy's of Reading, Pennsylvania, in 1927. Pomeroy's would remain in the Public Square location for the next sixty years. Over the course of its existence, it gradually became one of the most beloved and respected department stores in the entire Wyoming Valley.

Jonas Long's Sons' loss in Scranton was Ike Oppenheim's gain. In a brilliant display of business acumen and a penchant for taking big risks, he cemented his place in local business circles as a force to be reckoned with. In keeping with his ambitious personality, Oppenheim immediately set out to make the now former Jonas Long's Sons Building into a thoroughly modern department store. He constructed a large warehouse directly behind the store soon after its purchase.[113] The two buildings were connected via an underground tunnel. This tunnel was used to transport associates and merchandise to and from the store. The warehouse also enabled the company to buy merchandise in bulk. The savings from this practice were then passed along to the customer in the form of lower prices. The complex's boiler plant was also modernized, having been completely moved and rebuilt to make room for the warehouse.[114] Later, as the needs of the store outgrew the warehouse, much larger warehousing and garage facilities were purchased at 230 Cliff Street, which served the Dry for the remainder of its existence.

While the entire store complex received a complete overhaul, the main store received the most attention by far. Led by architect Edward H. Davis, the entire building was completely renovated at a cost of $200,000.[115] The atrium that extended through all four floors was closed and the floors were solidified to create additional sales space.[116] This change was made possible by advances made in lighting technology. Oppenheim took full advantage of these advances by installing a new lighting system of both the gas and electric type that brightly and consistently illuminated the sales floors at all hours of the business day. It also spotlighted the merchandise, thereby making it more attractive to passing customers. Other improvements to the store's physical plant included new, modern steam heating and a vacuum air cleaning system installed by local firm Gaylord & Eitapenc. On the street floor, the small existing balcony was extended so that it ran the full length of two sides of the building, creating a mezzanine floor to house additional departments, offices and a tearoom with fountain service. On the exterior, the street floor display windows were altered and modernized so that they now created an unbroken line of portals between entrances. These new windows gave the store's visual display team the capability of creating innovative merchandising spectacles that could rival not only The Globe's but also those of stores in much larger

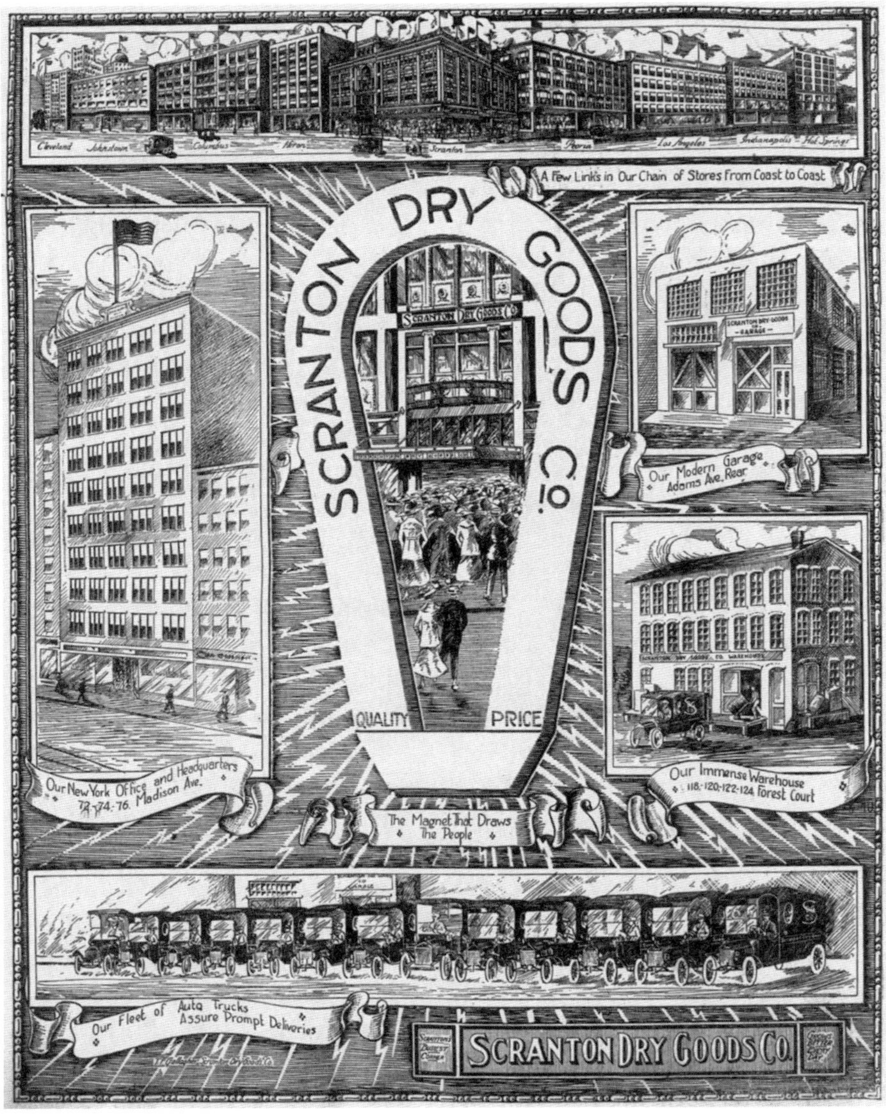

Above: When the new Scranton Dry Goods Company opened in 1917, the store took out full-page ads in local papers such as this one to showcase its new mammoth store building. *Author's collection.*

Opposite: 1917 portrait of the Scranton Dry Goods Company's expansive street floor. *Author's collection.*

metropolises. Above the windows, the phrases "WE BUY FOR LESS" and "WE SELL FOR LESS" were emblazoned across the façade. As customers entered and exited the store, they were sheltered from the elements by new, elegant entrance marquees that displayed the company name. Several of the windows on the upper floors were replaced with frosted panes that were etched with elegant designs and a stylized logo consisting of the company's initials. To top it all off, two gigantic signs were added to the rooftop on both the Lackawanna and Wyoming Avenue sides of the building. These signs were illuminated at night; its giant gold letters shining, glittering and proudly proclaiming to all those in the Electric City that this was indeed the Scranton Dry Goods Company.

With all the additional space afforded by the new building and the many alterations and improvements made to it, Ike Oppenheim was able to add many new departments to his store, as well as greatly enlarging those that already existed. Among these were a delicatessen, an expanded men's shop, an extensive toy department and a sanitary grocery store.[117] As a convenience to his customers, Oppenheim purchased fourteen delivery vehicles that enabled merchandise to be delivered directly to the customer's doorstep.[118] Thanks to the new warehouse and delivery system, an order could be processed, placed on the truck and be on the customer's doorstep all in the same day.[119] The new service was greatly appreciated by customers and extended the company's business to those who might otherwise not have ventured into the store.

With his new store improved and enlarged in every way, Ike Oppenheim formally opened the new Scranton Dry Goods Company to the public on July 18, 1917.[120] With an army of five hundred associates ready to serve the people, the giant emporium was practically an instant success and proved Oppenheim's hunch on the location to be correct. His store was now positioned as one of the largest and most beautiful department stores in the Northeast and a worthy competitor to The Globe. Throngs of customers pushed through the revolving doors to view the expansive and modern sales floors chock full of the latest merchandise.

The new store was indeed gigantic by the standards of the day, but by 1925, it too proved to be cramped quarters for the growing Dry store. More space would have to be added. Oppenheim looked to lease the parcel next door on Wyoming Avenue, but that space was already host to another legendary Scranton retail establishment, Lewis & Reilly. Lewis & Reilly was a longtime shoe store in the city, and being highly successful, its owners were not keen on leaving their prime location next to a thriving department store anchor. Fortunately, Ike Oppenheim's business genius came to the rescue. In another bold move, Oppenheim struck a deal with the president of Lewis & Reilly that behooved both companies and allowed them to achieve their goals with minimal disruption to business. The deal stated that the current building that Lewis & Reilly occupied would be demolished in favor of a new eight-story structure. There would be no interruption in business, as Lewis & Reilly would move to temporary quarters at 124 Wyoming Avenue. The land on which Lewis & Reilly stood would be leased by Oppenheim's company, which would also provide the financial capital for construction. The shoe store would occupy the street floor and basement while the Dry would lease the other floors for additional sales, stock and office space. Thus, Oppenheim's deal with Lewis & Reilly fulfilled the latter's wish to stay put while simultaneously allowing for the former's large-scale expansion plan.

Keeping Lewis & Reilly in place benefited Oppenheim's dry goods establishment in another way, as the venerable shoe store's slogan "always busy" proved to be very true indeed. Lewis & Reilly was a beloved institution in and of itself, and the store commanded a loyal following. Synonymous with quality footwear, it also held the distinction of being one of the few large businesses in the area that was owned and operated by a woman, Jennie Lewis Evans. Due to the social constraints of the day, female business executives were a rarity in the late nineteenth and early twentieth centuries. Jennie Lewis was born in Carmarthenshire, Wales, and immigrated to Scranton in 1868 with her parents, Reese J. and Ann Jones Lewis.[121] Her father worked as a miner until his death in 1887. While receiving her education in area public schools, Jennie Lewis decided on a career in business at an early age.[122] After completing her education, Lewis landed her first job at

Goldsmith Brothers as a clerk.[123] Lewis quietly and carefully observed all aspects of store operations and promised herself that she could become a successful merchant in her own right.[124] She remained in their employ until 1888.[125] That year, she partnered with David M. Reilly and Mary Davies and established a store at 114 Wyoming Avenue. Trading under the name Lewis, Reilly & Davies, the partners nurtured and grew their business with hard work, effective management and good business sense. After twelve years, Mary Davies sold her interests to her partners and retired from the business in 1900. The store became one of the most prosperous of its kind in the city, and the two remaining partners continued to share in its prosperity until April 1911, when D.M. Reilly left as well.[126] Jennie Lewis and her brother, Attorney W.R. Lewis, purchased Reilly's interest, but as part of an agreement between both sides, the company name remained unchanged. Despite D.M. Reilly no longer being part of the firm, Lewis was wise not to change its name, as it had gained a great deal of respect and loyalty among local shoppers. Lewis was so successful as a top business executive that she earned a reputation as Scranton's leading businesswoman."[127] In addition to her role as store president, Jennie Lewis served as a member of the Scranton Chamber of Commerce, director of the YMCA, charter member and honorary president of the Quota Club of Scranton and as a charter member of the Plymouth Congregational Church, where she served as president of its Ladies Aid Society. In 1909, Lewis fell in love and married a fellow shoe merchant and Welsh immigrant, Elias E. Evans.[128]

A photograph of the Lewis & Reilly shoe store along with its famous slogan, "ALWAYS BUSY," emblazoned across its gleaming terra-cotta façade. *Courtesy of the Lackawanna Historical Society.*

Evans owned and operated the highly successful firm of D.D. Evans and Company, which was in the city's Hyde Park section.[129] Later, he became senior partner in the firm of Evans & Powell, as well as being active in the religious and educational aspects of that part of the city.[130] Jennie Lewis Evans continued in her role as president of Lewis & Reilly until her death on December 17, 1940. Lewis's brother and later her nieces and nephews carried on her legacy until Lewis & Reilly closed in late 1986.

With the agreement to build a new building on the site of Lewis & Reilly, the old Victorian store structure it formerly occupied was demolished in April 1925. In its place rose a modern, gleaming eight-story colossus that was designed by architects Edward Davis and George M.D. Lewis. Completed in 1926, the Chicago School architecture, cream-colored terra-cotta cladding and elaborate neo-gothic details found in the window casings, cornices and door frames rivaled Lansing Holden's original corner building in beauty and scale. More importantly, the project accomplished the Dry's expansion plan by bringing the store's size to 185,728 square feet, thereby surpassing The Globe and officially making the Dry Scranton's largest store.[131]

In addition to the new building, the entire store received a complete renovation in which all departments were given more space and new departments were added. One of the conveniences designed into the new structure were cold storage vaults for the preservation of products made from animal fur.[132] The first of their kind in the city, the vaults proved popular with customers and further enhanced the Dry's reputation as a progressive department store. Other improvements included new lighting, floors, carpets and painting, which gave the store a contemporary look. The two structures were seamlessly integrated on the upper floors by the removal of interior walls and much redecoration.

As previously stated, the sudden abundance of space afforded Oppenheim the opportunity to add and enlarge many departments, some of which were unknown to the city until that point. This was similar to how the move to the corner of Lackawanna and Wyoming Avenues in 1917 had caused the company to grow exponentially in a relatively short period of time. One new department that was added as part of the expansion was a book department and lending library.[133] This was in direct response to The Globe's addition of a book department and library and further enabled the Dry to match its archrival in services and merchandise offerings. Next to the book department was a full bakery and candy department, the contents of which were prepared by the Dry's staff in its own kitchens.

To provide a central location for customer inquiries, a service desk was installed on the street floor at which customers could ask questions, receive directions and have gifts wrapped free of charge.[134] The expanded mezzanine overlooking the street floor was revamped to provide room for an optical center, a radio center, a tire and automotive department, the employment office and a customer waiting room.[135] The Tea Room on the mezzanine was also completely remodeled in a gold color scheme and now featured Pullman-style tables with marble tops.[136] The soda fountain was given its own space in an alcove of the restaurant.[137] Upstairs, fine china and cutlery were moved to their own space in an adjacent building on Lackawanna Avenue that the Dry had leased. A doorway had been created between the two structures on the second floor to provide access to the new annex.[138] On the fourth floor, the furniture department received a unique feature in the form of a full-size five-room apartment.[139] The apartment's rooms would be used to display furniture sets in a way that would give customers an idea of what they would look like in a typical home setting. Most of the other departments throughout the store were either enlarged, revamped or both. For the health and safety of the store's guests and staff, a working hospital was added along with a full-time nurse who was on staff during operating hours.[140] In addition to all the changes to the sales floors and employee areas, the store's physical plant also received a major overhaul that included the installation of a new sprinkler system.[141]

For the store's female shoppers, the beauty parlor on the second floor, which enjoyed the distinction of being the first of its kind in a Scranton department store, was remodeled and enlarged.[142] Now an ultramodern facility, a 1926 trade paper stated that "new apparatus has been installed and time required for hair waving and shampooing has been reduced by half."[143] As part of this renovation, a full ladies' lounge was installed where female customers could relax, recharge and socialize with fellow customers while waiting for their appointments.[144]

While Ike Oppenheim spared no expense in creating the most welcoming and comfortable shopping atmosphere possible, he did not forget his employees when the expansion project was being carried out. For the welfare of the Dry's staff members, a new cafeteria, locker room and men's smoking room were constructed on the sixth and eighth floors. The eighth-floor rooftop was given over to a garden and recreation area where employees could spend their breaks outdoors while enjoying breathtaking views of the city and surrounding landscape.[145] For those days when weather conditions were less than favorable, part of the recreation area was glass enclosed.[146] On the third floor, a new office was designed for Ike Oppenheim and top store executives that featured exquisite white oak paneling, lush oriental carpeting and a gothic-themed gas fireplace, above which hung a portrait of Ike's mother, Regina. The balance of the new building's space on the seventh and eighth floors provided space for stock and merchandise processing spaces. From here, a large spiral shaft twisted its way through the building all the way to the basement. This vertical shaft provided a quick means of transporting merchandise from the stock areas down to the sales floors.

Perhaps the most exciting addition to the Dry during this period was its new escalators in 1924. Known initially as "moving stairs," this relatively new invention was the first of its kind in Scranton, and there was much hoopla surrounding their installation. The store placed several advertisements in area newspapers espousing the convenience and modernity of the escalators and that their addition was another example of the forward-thinking mindset that led the Scranton Dry Goods Company. The company even held a party especially for children so they could learn to safely ride the moving stairs and allay any fears the youngsters may have had.[147] The store sweetened the deal by offering each child a lollipop after they completed a ride up to the fourth floor and back down to the first.[148] The "Kiddie Escalator Party" was held on October 4, 1924, and marked the formal opening of the escalators to the public.[149] Scores of area children showed up at the store eager to ride this much ballyhooed contraption. The escalators were an instant hit and became a popular attraction in the area. Area children viewed them as something akin to an amusement park ride while adults appreciated their novelty and convenience. Built by the Otis Elevator Company, the escalators were constructed almost entirely out of wood, including the cleated steps. Former customer Addie Warenzak remembers that the stairs' jumbo cleats would cause "ladies' high heels to get stuck in between the ridges."[150] She went on to say that "when they [customers] stepped off the escalator, their shoe didn't go with them."[151] Nevertheless, the escalators became an integral part of the store's image and were there to stay. While some were wary of this new form of technology and preferred to use the store's three passenger elevators to travel through the store, most customers embraced the moving stairs. It was estimated that the Dry's escalators could safely, comfortably and quickly trundle a maximum of 6,000 people per hour throughout the store's four floors.[152] A 1926 count broke records by showing that 5,311 shoppers used the first-floor escalator in just one hour.[153]

A photograph of the Dry's new Otis escalators with their wooden sides and treads. *Courtesy of the New York State Library, Albany.*

After decades of unabated success, the Dry endured its first major tragedy on February 20, 1954, when Ike Oppenheim passed away.[154] Gone was Scranton's energetic merchant prince and the guiding force behind the company's phenomenal success. His thoroughly American success story was recounted in several articles that also touted his philanthropy, kindness, faith and love for his community.[155] In his honor, the Dry was closed on the day of his funeral so that his associates could attend the services. Afterward, those left minding the store—namely, Ike's widow, Constance, and his sons, Ellis and Richard—were tasked with filling his shoes and carrying on his legacy. Constance Oppenheim assumed the role of president of the store while her elder son, Ellis, became vice-president. Constance's younger son, Richard, became the company's secretary-treasurer. Despite the enormous gravity of his loss, this transition of power was relatively seamless. The Dry had always been a family business, and Ike's family had been working with and learning from him from the very beginning.

As the leaders of one of Scranton's largest retailing firms, Constance Oppenheim and her sons carried on the family patriarch's legacy by continuing to remain competitive, generous and innovative. In 1951, the store had expanded yet again with the addition of two penthouse floors on top of the original corner structure.[156] Also that year, additional escalators were installed, the business offices were consolidated and the entire store was completely renovated.[157]

SCRANTON
CITY WIDE
SALE DAYS
SCRANTON
SALES
DAYS
SCRANTON
SALES
DAYS

Opposite, top: The Scranton Dry Goods as it appeared during one of its famous "Oppenheim Days" sale events. *From the Mark Boock Collection. Courtesy of Greg Boock.*

Opposite, bottom: Shoppers jam the Scranton Dry Goods' street floor in search of deals during one of Scranton's "City-Wide Sale Days" events in the 1950s. *Author's collection.*

Above: The newly expanded and renovated Scranton Dry Goods Company. *From the Mark Boock Collection. Courtesy of Greg Boock.*

The Dry's remarkable growth and investment reflected its commitment to Scranton. In 1955, Mayor James T. Hanlon publicly praised the store when he said that it represented "the kind of faith Scranton needs most."[158] When the store celebrated its fiftieth anniversary in February 1962, the Oppenheim family reaffirmed its dedication to the store and to the city that it called home.[159] As it was the Dry's golden jubilee, a gala ball was held at the nearby Hotel Casey, where the store's leadership played host to the store's working family of associates.[160] By that time, the Dry's workforce numbered over 650 employees, which ballooned to approximately 900 during the holiday season.[161]

I.E.'s sons, Richard (*left*) and Ellis Sr. (*right*), stand beside their mother, Constance, in the store's executive office as part of a celebration of the company's fiftieth anniversary in business in 1962. A portrait of their father, I.E. Oppenheim, can be seen in the background. *Courtesy of the Oppenheim family.*

Enduring tremendous change, expansion and tragedy, both The Globe and the Dry experienced their fair share of ups and downs. Through it all, they emerged as two of Pennsylvania's finest stores by the mid-twentieth century. It seemed like nothing could stop their escalating success.

3

PARKING SPACE

As World War II came to an end in 1945 and America's soldiers returned home, there was a newfound enthusiasm for consumer spending across the nation. After a generation of economic hardship brought on by the Great Depression and two world wars, Americans were utterly tired of austerity. Seeking to dust off the sorrows of war and enjoy the stability of peacetime, they crowded the country's downtowns looking for grand, gaudy entertainment through motion pictures, live performances, food and shopping. America's newfound status as the only economic powerhouse left in the world that had not had its industry decimated in the war created thousands of well-paying blue-collar jobs. The pay and benefits of these jobs were further enhanced by the simultaneous rise of labor unions and expanded federal programs such as the G.I. Bill of Rights. Flush with expendable income, American spending in the 1950s drove a booming economy that saw the advent of what is known as the "American Dream"—that is, the American middle class was now able to attain items that were previously unaffordable to them such as cars, new furniture, expensive clothes and suburban houses. Production companies responded to this economic excess in kind. Hence, cars became garishly large and received large tailfins, bright colors and acres of chrome. Women's fashions of the era also reflected the public taste for bright pastel colors and modern design. Interior design eschewed Victorian formality and detail in favor of clean lines and space-age modernism. The country was changing rapidly in the mid-twentieth century and, while The Globe and the Dry were enjoying the economic boom that this change created, it was clear that both stores would have to make significant changes if they were to keep pace with the seismic shifts taking place in American society.

Prior to World War II, a great number of Americans used public transportation to get around the cities in which they lived and worked. Due to many families' inability to afford cars, people used trolleys, buses, taxis and, for farther distances, trains. For the most part, families settled in cities to make the commute to and from work, church and business establishments as simple and least expensive as possible. As previously stated, the world dominance of American manufacturing, the strengthening of labor unions and the rise of the middle class after World War II enabled ordinary families to purchase automobiles. The modern notion of suburban living was born out of this era. Young couples, newly mobile in their cars, were able to move farther away from cities and into growing housing developments in the rural areas surrounding them. This was amplified throughout the 1940s, 1950s and 1960s by the construction of highways and expressways such as the Scranton-Carbondale Highway and the North and Central Scranton Expressways as well as the Pennsylvania Turnpike and Interstate Highway System. These new roadways created several easy and fast ways to travel to and from the city. More and more residents moved from Scranton and built homes in neighboring villages such as Clarks Summit, Dalton, Dallas, Dunmore, Dickson City, Jermyn, Eynon and Jessup. This population shift gave rise to an ever-increasing threat to Scranton's downtown retail establishments: the suburban shopping center. Many examples of this new concept in retail began popping up throughout the 1950s and early 1960s as the distance between potential customers and downtown Scranton grew greater. One example was the construction of the Abington Shopping Center in Clarks Summit, which was begun in 1958. When completed, it featured a Grant's discount department store, a full-service Acme supermarket and several smaller stores and restaurants. Other shopping centers sprang up in Dunmore and the South Side and Green Ridge sections of Scranton. One of the most successful local shopping malls in the early 1960s was the Keyser-Oak Shopping Center. Officially opened on May 24, 1961, the one-story, U-shaped shopping complex was built outside of the city's center and featured 160,000 square feet of retail space that included Towers Department Store, Woolworth's, Food Fair Supermarket, Thrift Drug and a host of smaller shops that wrapped around a large parking lot. It was an instant hit among local shoppers. These centers, also called "strip malls," offered several advantages to shoppers such as the ability

A view of Lackawanna Avenue in the 1950s. *Author's collection.*

Parked cars fill both sides of busy Wyoming Avenue in the early 1970s. *Author's collection.*

to avoid city traffic and access to acres of free parking. It was the latter that posed the greatest threat to The Globe and the Dry. Both stores were built around the widespread use of public transportation. To this end, a bus stop was installed in front of the main entrance of each of the two stores. The increasing popularity of personal vehicles as well as the use of buses had put an end to the service that gave Scranton its nickname. Amid music from a live band and crowds gathered to bid it farewell, the electric trolley made its last run in the Electric City on December 18, 1954. With change at their doorstep, neither store had the ability to accommodate large numbers of customers looking to park their own cars near them. Scranton attempted to rectify this by building parking lots throughout the downtown area. This, however, was not enough to compete with suburban convenience. To stay competitive, The Globe and the Dry needed a more ambitious large-scale response.

The Globe: Twisting and Turning

The Globe responded first. In 1954, bold plans were drawn-up for a multilevel ultramodern parking facility that would extend the first floor and basement levels of the store all the way back to Penn Avenue. It would also create a separate entrance on Spruce Street, now known as Biden Street, giving the store convenient entryways on three major thoroughfares in the middle of the city's busy downtown.

Upon the announcement of The Globe's plans, the store soon faced legal opposition. The owner of several buildings along Center Street claimed that closing part of a small street known as Oakford Court to build The Globe's garage would obstruct access to their properties. Although it did delay the project, the resulting litigation and subsequent appeal were adjudicated and resolved in The Globe's favor. The row of old buildings facing Penn Avenue was demolished, and construction commenced soon after. The project attracted a great deal of attention, and The Globe's management had peepholes installed in the temporary walls surrounding the construction site so passersby could get a glimpse of the project's progress.

Designed by architect F. Clifton Pearce, the new addition was slated to cost $2.5 million and consist of a first floor and basement that were to be used as additional sales and stock space for the store.[162] In total, this added over 36,000 square feet of sales space that later became home to expanded and new departments such as books, music, pianos, photography, small electrics, major appliances, televisions, radios and a new 250-seat restaurant called the Charl-Mont. Below, the basement Budget Store was greatly expanded, and a new stock and delivery processing center was installed. The street level also housed a large garage that was used to house The Globe's fleet of delivery trucks. The sub-basement level of the Easy Park Garage contained space for overflow stock as well as new design studios where Globe artisans toiled to create new and exciting floor and window displays, including those that were shown at Christmastime.

Cars fill the spaces in front of The Globe during its 75th Anniversary Diamond Jubilee Sale in 1953. *Author's collection.*

Construction progresses on the helical parking ramp as part of The Globe's new Easy Park Garage. *Author's collection.*

Above the new, ultramodern store structure, four parking levels would be stacked on round, recessed concrete columns that, from the outside, gave the appearance that the floors were "floating" on air. All the levels, including the rooftop, could house a total of five hundred cars. It was thought that daily turnover would result in the garage handling upward of two thousand cars per day. In addition to creating parking space, the rooftop of the garage would also house The Globe's new garden center.

The Globe Easy Park garage and Penn Avenue addition formally opened on May 1, 1958. To access this futuristic facility, a unique helical parking ramp was built facing Spruce Street that reached each level and served both ascending and descending traffic. Despite its unique design, traversing the twisting spiral ramp was at times a nerve-racking experience, particularly for those drivers who were less than confident navigating the massive boat-like cars that dominated the nation's roadways at the time.

Despite the occasional nervous driver, the new self-service parkade was appropriately named the "Easy Park" Garage due to its connection to the main store building. This setup provided easy access to the store from all levels. With the new design, Globe shoppers would never have to brave the elements again if they did not wish to—that is, one could simply park their car in the covered garage and walk directly into the store. Conversely, customers exiting the store could walk directly out of the store to their cars and drive out without ever being outside. Excited to advertise this convenience, the store's talented public relations department came up with a slogan for the store: "Park, shop, and dine under one roof." Even The Globe's credit cards bore the new slogan. To commemorate the event, the store had bronze and wood plaques created that bore an image of the garage along with its new logo: a hexagonal sign emblazoned with bold letters reading "Easy Park." This hexagonal sign was also suspended from the Spruce Street entrance of the garage. The Penn Avenue side received a larger sign that simply said "THE GLOBE" in bold red letters arranged vertically. As The Globe had some nighttime hours, especially during the holidays, both signs as well as the entire garage were brightly illuminated.

In addition to the garage, The Globe built a new automotive center adjacent to the new structure at 134 Penn Avenue. The Globe Auto Center dealt in tires and various supplies needed to maintain automobiles. This and the new Easy Park building proved that The Globe had fully embraced the automobile age. Customers responded well to the new garage. By 1969, the Easy Park had safely accommodated over four million cars.

Left: A 1958 Globe advertisement showcasing the store's new Easy Park facility. *Author's collection.*

Right: Friendly rivals. The Scranton Dry congratulates its archrival, The Globe, on the completion of the Easy Park Garage while simultaneously promoting the impending construction of its own Car Park on North Washington Avenue. *Author's collection.*

The Dry: You Take the Wheel

The Dry, which lacked any form of parking facility in the immediate vicinity of the store, had to respond. It had to match its archrival across Wyoming Avenue if it hoped to stay competitive. As the Easy Park Garage took shape, The Globe would soon become a self-contained shopping center by giving its customers the ability to park, shop and dine under one roof.

The Dry's initial ideas were both ambitious and grandiose. In 1955, the Dry released plans for an impressive store expansion and modernization project that included a colossal parking structure to be constructed on the site of what was then the former JCPenney Department Store building in the 100 block of North Washington Avenue. JCPenney had closed its downtown location, and the Dry purchased its former digs to expand and, ironically, reestablish the store's presence on the street where it had been founded. On the JCPenney property, which was situated between the side entrance of Woolworth's and the main entrance of Neisner's in the Connell Building, the Dry intended to build a structure similar to the Easy Park garage. The Dry's garage, like The Globe's on Penn Avenue, would house additional sales space for the store on the first two floors while the six levels above would provide space for four hundred cars. Designed by Joseph H. Young, a partner in the architectural-engineering firm Gilboy, Bellante & Clauss, the plans were honored with an award from the nationally recognized architectural magazine *Progressive Architecture*.[163] Unlike The Globe, however, the new structure would not be directly connected to the store building due to the distance and positions of the two structures. To solve this, a garden court would be constructed above-ground to provide shoppers with a leisurely walk to the main store. Below, an underground tunnel would connect the main store with the new addition. There, customers would not need to worry about walking, as a moving walkway was to be installed to swiftly transport them.

As for the main store building, it was also to undergo a major overhaul. Outside, Lansing Holden's magnificent neoclassical façade was to be covered in an ultramodern sheath of aluminum screens and steel bars. Covering aging store structures in modern materials was a popular method at the time to disguise their true age. Local examples of this trend could be found in neighboring Wilkes-Barre where Pomeroy's and Fowler, Dick and Walker–The Boston Store had concealed their ornate Victorian faces with space-age plastic, chrome and ceramic tile. To expand the Dry's existing sales space, the fifth and sixth penthouse floors added in 1951 would be extended to cover the entire corner building.

As the project progressed, the Dry's plans were scaled back significantly. On North Washington Avenue, a significantly smaller three-hundred-car garage was planned that, with the exception of a garden center and a small pet shop that was added later, did not include additional sales space for the store. A rather simple vertical belt manlift connected all the parking levels and provided a quick means of transport for garage staff. In addition, there would be no underground moving walkway. Instead, a modest courtyard was created in the alleyway behind the store that included potted plants and painted footsteps on the ground to lead shoppers to the Dry's rear entrance. Additionally, the store's classic façade would be preserved as the aluminum screens were abandoned in favor of a more conservative

An artistic rendering of the Scranton Dry Car Park from a store advertisement highlighting the garage's convenient valet service. *Author's collection.*

renovation of the street floor display windows. As part of the makeover, the main level windows were framed in steel and surrounded by light-colored granite and dark green tile. The main entrances and marquees also received significant updates.

The new Scranton Dry Goods Company Car Park officially opened to the public in April 1959. Since the Dry could not claim to provide the same direct access to the store that The Globe had, it offered customers free valet service as an added convenience. The company placed advertisements espousing the virtues of the new service by saying, "It's so easy…it's so quick! Drive in…an attendant parks for you! And Scranton Dry Goods Car Park is located right in the center of the Scranton Shopping area!"[164] In practice, however, the service had mixed results. Customer Addie Warenzak remembers, "The Dry Goods hired teenagers to park cars for them. As you walked near their parking garage, you could hear squealing tires. The kids were racing the cars up and down the ramps!"[165]

Growing pains and initial customer hesitation notwithstanding, The Globe and the Dry successfully took bold action to combat the growing threat of the suburban shopping center. In so doing, they brought themselves into the modern age by catering to a customer base that now preferred to get around on their own wheels. While the overall efficacy of the garages is not certain, what is certain is that these expansion projects helped stave off the inevitable and extend the stores' existence in the city significantly.

4

THE FINEST IN CUISINE... THE MOST EXCELLENT IN SERVICE... THE ULTIMATE IN DINING

When most customers ventured downtown in the 1950s and 1960s, it was a daylong adventure. Shoppers often eagerly waited at locked doors for the stores' 10:00 a.m. opening and stayed in the city until they closed at 5:30 pm. On Thursdays, The Globe and the Dry stayed open until 9:00 p.m. To meet local demand, Monday night hours were later added as well as extended hours during peak shopping periods. Long before the era when stores stayed open late into the night or twenty-four hours, department stores maintained a business day that was relatively short by today's standards. On Sundays, all stores were closed per Pennsylvania's Blue Laws, which dictated that nonessential businesses would not be open in observance of the Christian Sabbath. While the holidays and changing shopping habits altered these hours periodically, this was the general schedule that Scranton's historic stores kept for most of their existence. To keep hungry customers from leaving the store to have breakfast, brunch, lunch or supper after a day of shopping, The Globe and the Dry offered several in-store dining options.

The Globe: Taste the Difference

While The Globe had maintained an in-store tearoom on the third floor since June 1924, it was in 1958 that it added the restaurant that most

A 1958 advertisement for the opening of The Charl-Mont Restaurant and candy counter. *Author's collection.*

Scrantonians remember most: the Charl-Mont. As part of the expansion project that included the Easy Park garage and the extension of the street floor and basement to Penn Avenue, the new addition was designed to include a brand-new, ultramodern restaurant with a full-service kitchen. A bakery and candy kitchen were also incorporated into the design. Located adjacent to the book department near the Penn Avenue entrance, the 250-seat Charl-Mont Restaurant catered to Globe shoppers looking for a bite to eat at lunchtime or a full-course dinner for later patrons. A breakfast menu was also available for early birds who could come into the restaurant at 8:00 a.m. and eat a meal prior to the store's opening time. This was possible thanks to the design of the new building, which included a separate entrance to the restaurant facing Penn Avenue. This was an added convenience for those who wanted to patronize the restaurant but avoid the hustle and bustle of the sales floor. Inside, the restaurant sported a modern and chic ambience with

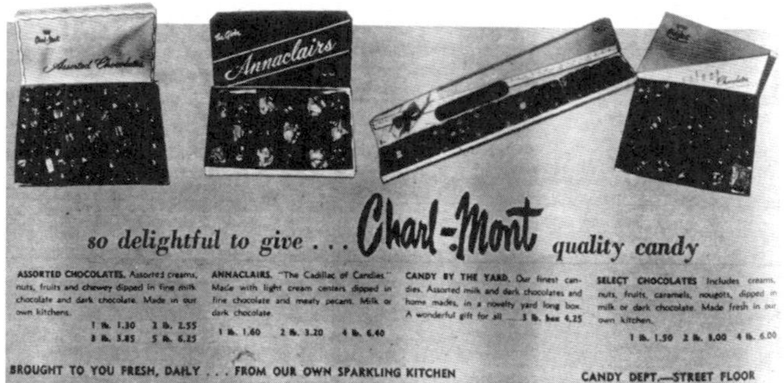

The Charl-Mont Restaurant. *Author's collection.*

clean lines, bright colors, comfortable seating and space-age lighting fixtures that hovered overhead. Various decorations and images lined the walls while the Penn Avenue side consisted of large windows that allowed natural light to flood the eatery. U-shaped counters surrounded by stools offered quick, convenient seating for those not looking for a full-dining experience. For that experience, both booths and traditional chairs surrounded tables that could seat four to six at a time.

The food at the Charl-Mont, both in the restaurant and at the adjacent bakery and candy counter, is remembered as being of superb quality. The Globe ensured this consistent reputation for good food and quality service by employing a team of workers who were dedicated to their craft. Professional chefs, complete with pristine white coats and chef's hats, cooked the traditional fare listed on the menu while courteous waitresses and waiters catered to the customers' every want and whim. As a visual representation of that reputation, the Charl-Mont logo featured a gold, seven-point crown with letters that spelled *quality* balancing on each point. Below, the phrase "taste the difference" completed the design.

When given a menu, a Charl-Mont patron had a plethora of dishes to choose from at very reasonable prices. In 1976, diners could help themselves to a cup of homemade soup or "be the Architect of your own salad from our 21-item soup, salad, and bread bar."[166] They could also choose from one of several luncheon suggestions that might include "Baked Macaroni Au Gratin, topped with a tangy tomato sauce, garden fresh peas" or "Baked Salisbury Steak" served with "Bermuda Onion Sauce, whipped potatoes, and glazed carrots."[167] Both dishes could be purchased for only $1.29. While the Charl-Mont offered many choices to its patrons, perhaps the most fondly remembered food item was the steamship round of beef, sliced to order by an immaculately dressed chef stationed in one corner of the restaurant. Heat lamps positioned above the cutting station ensured the beef would be piping hot when slices were placed on customers' plates. When asked about the Charl-Mont's signature dish, head chef Gus Bensing stated that "U.S. Choice beef rounds weighing between 75 and 85 pounds are roasted at 250° for 8½ to 9½ hours. The natural juice of these rounds is then used to make the gravy which adds greatly to the flavor of your sandwich or platter."[168]

Outside the Charl-Mont Restaurant itself, one would find the Charl-Mont bakery and candy shop. The bakery was known for its delicious cookies, cakes, cupcakes, jelly rolls, lemon tarts and various other baked items. If one desired, the bakery could even create a beautiful wedding cake. The candy counter, located just behind the street floor escalators, is also remembered for its "Chocolate Melt-A-Ways," "Cold-Water Fudge," pecan rolls, pretzels, caramels, salted nuts, jellies and "Annaclairs." A Charl-Mont exclusive, Annaclairs consisted of a whipped vanilla center covered in milk or dark chocolate and rolled in finely chopped walnuts or pecans. During the holidays, special candy was produced, such as chocolate bunnies at Easter and heart-shaped boxes of goodies for Valentine's Day. Both the candy and the baked goods were made in The Globe's sixth-floor candy kitchens and bakery by the store's own staff of professional candymakers and bakers. It was then shipped downstairs to the sales floor via freight elevator.

Although many residents of Northeastern Pennsylvania remember the Charl-Mont experience as being unique to The Globe Store, it was actually a subsidiary of the Price Candy Company of Kansas City, Missouri.

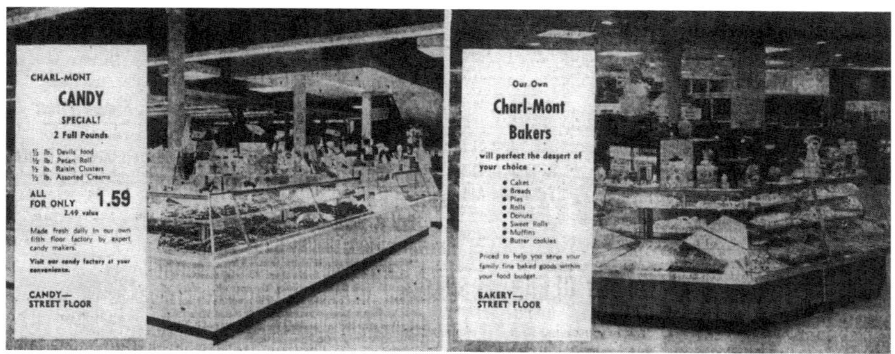

Advertisements showcasing the Charl-Mont candy counter (*left*) and bakery (*right*). *Author's collection.*

Founded in 1913, Price Candy Company provided restaurant, tearoom and fountain services to various establishments under the Charl-Mont banner. Hence, one could find Charl-Mont restaurants in various department stores around the country, including Gimbels of Milwaukee, Wisconsin; Stripling's of Fort Worth, Texas; Kilpatrick's of Omaha, Nebraska; Davison's of Atlanta, Georgia; and Emery, Bird, Thayer of Kansas City, Missouri. Although its origins are ambiguous, it is highly probable that the restaurant's unique, French-sounding name is a combination of the names of the Price Candy Company's founder and president, Charles H. Price and Harry F. Montgomery, respectively.[169] That is, the moniker is a blend of CHARLes and MONTgomery.

If the Charl-Mont was known for full-course meals and formal service, its subterranean counterpart, the Green Room, had a reputation for light fare, snacks and fast-food-like service. Located in The Globe's basement Budget Store just off the main stairway, this small lunchroom provided a quick stop for hurried shoppers or those looking for a simpler, lower-priced meal. The name was inspired by the room's green themed décor. On March 12, 1980, the Green Room officially became Spuds. Just as the name suggests, the eatery dealt almost exclusively in baked potatoes that could be customized with a variety of toppings, advertised as "meals with a peel." Shoppers were invited to create their very own "V.I.P.—Very Important Potato." The grand opening declared the newly themed restaurant as "unique in N.E. Penna. [*sic*], Spuds features giant baked potato entrees stuffed with 106 possible combinations of toppings, plus homemade soup and salad bar."[170]

THE GREEN ROOM

The Globe's Green Room. *Author's collection.*

The Charl-Mont restaurant, bakery and candy shop, along with the Green Room/Spuds in the Budget Store, helped give customers a pleasant and satisfying shopping experience. Together, they cemented The Globe's reputation as a business of excellence.

The Dry: A Room with a View

As The Globe expanded and changed its eateries over the years, the Dry's remained consistent throughout its history. From the time of the store's big move to the corner of Lackawanna and Wyoming Avenues in 1917, Ike Oppenheim offered his customers a modern and inviting place to relax and have something to eat. Initially, the Dry's restaurant consisted of little more than a soda fountain located near the escalators on the first floor.

Later, it was enlarged and moved to the store's mezzanine level, where it offered sweeping views of the hustle and bustle on the street floor below. In 1926, the Dry's Fountain Tea Room was described as "finished in gold and the tables are arranged in Pullman type with figured marble tops."[171] Hence, this early décor led to the restaurant being initially dubbed the Gold Room. This name did not last, and most remember the eatery by its longest-lived name, the Tea Room. A holdover from the initial dining area, one of the most popular features of the mezzanine Tea Room was the soda fountain, which was built into a small alcove. Another popular feature was the addition of air-conditioning in the 1930s, used as a marketing tool and heavily promoted in the Tea Room's menus. Customers were told that "the air you are breathing is fresh air: air conditioning, the newest feature of our Tea Room is designed to protect the health and promote the comfort of our patrons."[172] The customer's health was also considered when placing food items on the menu. On May 26, 1937, for example, Tea Room patrons could order a chilled tomato filled with assorted vegetables with bran muffins or assorted fruit salad with cream cheese and a pineapple sandwich on brown bread. Both meals could be had for only thirty-five cents. Those looking for something more substantial could have Baked Lamb Loaf with vegetable sauce, scalloped potatoes, buttered peas, hot rolls and one's choice of coffee or a pot of tea. Again, in 1937, one could order these full meals for thirty-five cents. One of the most popular dishes at the Dry was the Chicken Croquettes. Resting on a heaping bed of mashed potatoes, smothered in gravy and served with a vegetable and a roll, this meal is commonly associated with the Tea Room and is fondly remembered by former customers.

In addition to the luncheon and dinner specials offered daily, the typical fare of tea sandwiches, salads, soups and desserts was always available. Tea sandwiches were a holdover from an era when Victorian women would gather to enjoy a light, dainty brunch. A variety of these small finger sandwiches could be ordered, including cucumber, chicken salad and cream cheese on date nut bread. As they were still listed as available in a 1964 Dry Goods menu, the Tea Room continued to cater to the "ladies who lunch" well after many other restaurants and diners had abandoned or forgotten these offerings. Those looking for something sweet after their meal would not be disappointed. The Tea Room offered a variety of desserts, including "Ski Hi Strawberry Chiffon," "Boston Cream Cake" or an "Ice Cream Ball with Butterscotch Sauce." In 1964, all these delectable dishes could be purchased for a quarter. The Dry further enticed patrons to indulge their sweet tooth with a pyramided, revolving dessert table that created a focal point for the room and attractively displayed glistening strawberries, luscious lemon pie and fudge brownies covered in flowing hot chocolate sauce.

Although in many ways the Dry adhered to its old-fashioned practices, it did update and modernize its restaurant several times throughout its existence. Perhaps the most dramatic update of the mezzanine eatery came in 1967 when the Tea Room was completely renovated. Modern furniture was added along with new carpeting, paint, wall coverings and lighting fixtures. By that time, the restaurant consisted of two main dining rooms that were divided by the store's escalators and could accommodate a total of 270 diners. The Executive Room, located on the left side, was "tastefully appointed with coral tables and chairs to pickup [*sic*] the coral poppies on the green background wallcovering."[173] On the right side of the escalators, patrons could dine in the Blue Room, so named because of its primarily white décor against blue walls. A royal blue carpet completed the theme. An additional private dining room was available for reservation by those looking to conduct business meetings, charitable events or parties.

Oppposite: An advertisement for the Dry's mezzanine Tea Room. *From the* Scranton Tribune, *July 18, 1948. Author's collection.*

Right: The cover of a 1964 Scranton Dry Goods Company Restaurant menu. *Author's collection.*

Below: The Scranton Dry Goods Company Restaurant menu from May 22, 1964. *Author's collection.*

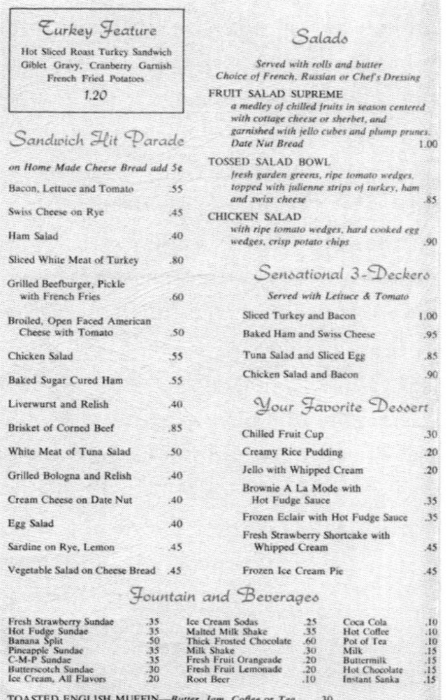

Turkey Feature

Hot Sliced Roast Turkey Sandwich
Giblet Gravy, Cranberry Garnish
French Fried Potatoes
1.20

Sandwich Hit Parade

on Home Made Cheese Bread add 5¢

Bacon, Lettuce and Tomato	.55
Swiss Cheese on Rye	.45
Ham Salad	.40
Sliced White Meat of Turkey	.80
Grilled Beefburger, Pickle with French Fries	.60
Broiled, Open Faced American Cheese with Tomato	.50
Chicken Salad	.55
Baked Sugar Cured Ham	.55
Liverwurst and Relish	.40
Brisket of Corned Beef	.85
White Meat of Tuna Salad	.50
Grilled Bologna and Relish	.40
Cream Cheese on Date Nut	.40
Egg Salad	.40
Sardine on Rye, Lemon	.45
Vegetable Salad on Cheese Bread	.45

Salads

Served with rolls and butter
Choice of French, Russian or Chef's Dressing

FRUIT SALAD SUPREME
a medley of chilled fruits in season centered with cottage cheese or sherbet, and garnished with jello cubes and plump prunes. Date Nut Bread 1.00

TOSSED SALAD BOWL
fresh garden greens, ripe tomato wedges, topped with julienne strips of turkey, ham and swiss cheese .85

CHICKEN SALAD
with ripe tomato wedges, hard cooked egg wedges, crisp potato chips .90

Sensational 3-Deckers

Served with Lettuce & Tomato

Sliced Turkey and Bacon	1.00
Baked Ham and Swiss Cheese	.95
Tuna Salad and Sliced Egg	.85
Chicken Salad and Bacon	.90

Your Favorite Dessert

Chilled Fruit Cup	.30
Creamy Rice Pudding	.20
Jello with Whipped Cream	.20
Brownie A La Mode with Hot Fudge Sauce	.35
Frozen Eclair with Hot Fudge Sauce	.35
Fresh Strawberry Shortcake with Whipped Cream	.45
Frozen Ice Cream Pie	.45

Fountain and Beverages

Fresh Strawberry Sundae	.35	Ice Cream Sodas	.25	Coca Cola	.10
Hot Fudge Sundae	.35	Malted Milk Shake	.35	Hot Coffee	.10
Banana Split	.50	Thick Frosted Chocolate	.60	Pot of Tea	.10
Pineapple Sundae	.35	Milk Shake	.30	Milk	.15
C-M-P Sundae	.35	Fresh Fruit Orangeade	.20	Buttermilk	.15
Butterscotch Sundae	.30	Fresh Fruit Lemonade	.20	Hot Chocolate	.15
Ice Cream, All Flavors	.20	Root Beer	.10	Instant Sanka	.15

TOASTED ENGLISH MUFFIN—*Butter, Jam, Coffee or Tea* .30

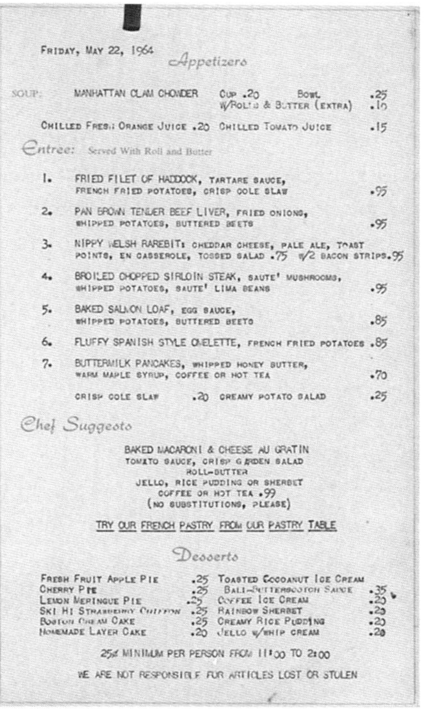

FRIDAY, MAY 22, 1964

Appetizers

SOUP: MANHATTAN CLAM CHOWDER CUP .20 BOWL .25
W/ROLLS & BUTTER (EXTRA) .10

CHILLED FRESH ORANGE JUICE .20 CHILLED TOMATO JUICE .15

Entree: Served With Roll and Butter

1. FRIED FILET OF HADDOCK, TARTARE SAUCE, FRENCH FRIED POTATOES, CRISP COLE SLAW .95
2. PAN BROWN TENDER BEEF LIVER, FRIED ONIONS, WHIPPED POTATOES, BUTTERED BEETS .95
3. NIPPY WELSH RAREBIT: CHEDDAR CHEESE, PALE ALE, TOAST POINTS, EN CASSEROLE, TOSSED SALAD .75 W/2 BACON STRIPS .95
4. BROILED CHOPPED SIRLOIN STEAK, SAUTE' MUSHROOMS, WHIPPED POTATOES, SAUTE' LIMA BEANS .95
5. BAKED SALMON LOAF, EGG SAUCE, WHIPPED POTATOES, BUTTERED BEETS .85
6. FLUFFY SPANISH STYLE OMELETTE, FRENCH FRIED POTATOES .85
7. BUTTERMILK PANCAKES, WHIPPED HONEY BUTTER, WARM MAPLE SYRUP, COFFEE OR HOT TEA .70

CRISP COLE SLAW .20 CREAMY POTATO SALAD .25

Chef Suggests

BAKED MACARONI & CHEESE AU GRATIN
TOMATO SAUCE, CRISP GARDEN SALAD
ROLL-BUTTER
JELLO, RICE PUDDING OR SHERBET
COFFEE OR HOT TEA .99
(NO SUBSTITUTIONS, PLEASE)

TRY OUR FRENCH PASTRY FROM OUR PASTRY TABLE

Desserts

FRESH FRUIT APPLE PIE	.25	TOASTED COCOANUT ICE CREAM	
CHERRY PIE	.25	BALI-BUTTERSCOTCH SAUCE	.35
LEMON MERINGUE PIE	.25	COFFEE ICE CREAM	.20
SKI HI STRAWBERRY CHIFFON	.25	RAINBOW SHERBET	.20
BOSTON CREAM CAKE	.25	CREAMY RICE PUDDING	.20
HOMEMADE LAYER CAKE	.20	JELLO W/WHIP CREAM	.20

25¢ MINIMUM PER PERSON FROM 11:00 TO 2:00

WE ARE NOT RESPONSIBLE FOR ARTICLES LOST OR STOLEN

It was also during the late 1960s that the Dry formally changed the eatery's name from the Tea Room to the Vista Restaurant. Named for the spectacular "vistas" that the two mezzanine rooms offered of the store's first floor, it was popular for customers to sit in a booth nearest the windows so that they could observe the ever-changing views below. Former customer Antoinette Altieri remembered that it was fun to sit in the booth nearest the escalators where one could wave at the customers gliding past.[174] The Vista title lasted until the store's demise over a decade later.

As was the case with The Globe's Charl-Mont restaurant, the Dry's restaurant was operated by an outside concessionaire. In the Dry's case, John F. Davis Co. operated the Tea Room and later the Vista Restaurant.[175] For many years, the restaurant was managed by Mario Genovese, whose family founded a popular food market in the area. Another longtime Tea Room manager and hostess was Evelyn Keeney, who began her career at the Dry in 1944 and was widely respected throughout the area for her professional opinion and expertise. John F. Davis Co. also operated the Dry's bakery and candy shop, which were both located on the street floor next to the escalators. While it is not clear when John F. Davis Co. took over the food operations at the store, it is known that the Dry advertised its sweet confections directly on its menus as "candy made fresh daily from recipes developed during our forty years of candy making!"[176] Other advertisements and store packaging furthered the Dry's homespun and homemade image by describing the candy as being made in their own candy kitchens and pastries being baked in ovens located right in the store. Regardless of who oversaw their creation, it cannot be disputed that the Dry's bakery and candy departments were immensely popular with locals who could not get enough of the multitude of sweets, chocolates, jellies and pastries that filled the glass display counters and produced delicious smells that wafted throughout the street floor.

What began as an attempt to keep customers inside the store evolved into legendary and integral departments that drew people in the door and greatly contributed to the fine reputations of both The Globe and the Dry. In many ways, the restaurants best represented the stores' quality, value and service. Beyond that, the dining experiences patrons had produced some of their most cherished memories of the stores and the people who accompanied them on their shopping adventures.

5

HOLIDAY HEADQUARTERS

The holidays were a magical time at the downtown department stores of yesteryear. Major retailers spent lavishly on elaborate decorations to grace all the sales floors of their grand emporiums. Santa Claus received quarters that could rival any frosted, glittering fantasy of his snowbound home at the North Pole, complete with a gold and velvet

Heavy traffic and holiday shoppers crowd Wyoming Avenue in this scene from a Christmas shopping season in the 1950s. *From the Mark Boock Collection. Courtesy of Greg Boock.*

throne for him to sit in. Likewise, the Easter Bunny felt right at home in his miniature version of April Valley. Overhead, festive music sung by the likes of Andy Williams, Bing Crosby, Nat King Cole and Dean Martin blared through the sound system. Many stores, most famously New York's R.H. Macy & Co., even sponsored parades in their home cities to welcome St. Nick. This over-the-top holiday cheer made good business sense. After all, department stores heavily depended on shoppers looking to purchase the perfect stocking stuffers and gifts to place under the tree to generate a major chunk of their yearly profits.

The Globe and the Dry both made earnest attempts each year to outdo each other with regard to their festive décor, elaborate window displays and, most importantly, their holiday sales figures. The battle that is most fondly remembered, however, is their attempt to convince local youngsters that their Santa Claus was indeed the real one. The other Santa across Wyoming Avenue was just one of his helpers. This yuletide one-upmanship forced both stores to be more and more creative each year, which in turn generated countless cherished memories for locals who were able to enjoy the candied fruits of the stores' labor.

The Globe: A Gift from the Globe Means More

The Globe is probably most fondly remembered at Christmastime. Its fancy façade decorations, Santa's World, holiday windows, Rudi Bears and busy departments inevitably tie it to many Scrantonians' recollections of holidays past. The Globe's staff went to great lengths to make its customers' holiday shopping experiences as pleasant and as magical as possible. As one approached the store, the first thing they saw was the glittering, glowing façade. Many stood on the sidewalks lining Wyoming Avenue in awe of the twinkling lights, giant pine trees, and swags of garland that festooned the top four floors of the storefront. In The Globe's early days, a massive decorative pipe organ graced the façade as well, which was used to "play" Christmas songs for the crowds traversing the street below. In reality, this music was being played by organists inside the store, often on the same model organs that were for sale in the street floor's piano and organ department. Later, the organ was eliminated in favor of a large banner that proudly proclaimed that "a gift from The Globe means more." That is, if one purchased a present from The Globe, it meant that they cared enough for the recipient to buy from the very best in town. As always, The Globe prided itself on its quality merchandise and solid reputation as a department store of distinction.

The Globe's holiday storefront usually debuted along with the Christmas windows the day after Thanksgiving. On Thanksgiving night, Addie Warenzak remembers that her family used to pile in the car and make a special trip to the city from their country home in nearby Dalton just to ride by the stores and see their intricate decorations.[177] Many who would normally utilize the Easy Park garage also made a special effort to walk down Wyoming Avenue to admire the windows, which often featured animated dolls, large reindeer, moving displays and a generous apportionment of pine and fake snow. Each year, these displays were first designed and developed

The Globe Store at Christmastime in December 1953. *Author's collection.*

in the sub-basement-level design studios before being placed in the windows for the holiday season. In front of the main entrance, the smell of roasted chestnuts permeated the crisp, cold air as a stand sold the holiday treat for many years.

Walking into the entrance lobby, customers would feel a warm blast of heat forcefully emanating from the vents above to combat the bitter cold outside. For several seasons, shoppers were greeted by an elaborate Nativity scene that was placed above the interior entrance doors. From the lobby, customers would swing through the store's iconic revolving doors and into a Christmas wonderland. Large twinkling Christmas trees, which reflected The Globe's exterior décor, towered above each display island. Swags of garland, wreaths and bows wrapped around the columns and stretched across the tin ceilings. As one ascended the escalators, they would find the same amount of attention had been given to all the store's upper shopping floors. Large poinsettia trees, for example, stood majestically against the backdrop of glittering dresses and expensive coats while collectible porcelain holiday villages were set up in the china and silver department. The Trim-

The Globe at Christmastime in the 1970s. *From the Mark Boock Collection. Courtesy of Greg Boock.*

A Christmas window at The Globe. *Author's collection.*

the-Home Shop on the third floor featured several Christmas trees decorated to sell elaborate ornaments as well as holiday figurines, woven stockings, Santa dolls and other Christmas decorations. In the toy department, Lionel trains whistled and clacked down their miniature tracks while area children watched in awe and excitement.

The staff responsible for these elaborate Christmas displays was led by James Hines, who was The Globe's visual and promotion director. Responsible for decorating over a quarter of a million square feet of floor space spread out over five floors, Hines's team was able to transform The Globe into a yuletide spectacle in a matter of days. After the store closed on Thanksgiving Eve, Hines and his staff would work almost nonstop until Black Friday morning, when the store opened again. In an interview given to Scranton-Wilkes-Barre PBS affiliate WVIA, former coat, suit and dress buyer Rita Lissefeld stated that to accommodate this tight, rigorous schedule, the decorating staff would eat their Thanksgiving meal in The Globe itself.[178]

The Globe and its staff members took great pride in the store's decorations. The December 1969 edition of the *Globe Trotter*, the in-store employee magazine, describes the great effort that went into the store's décor and how its associates should treat holiday shoppers:

A large Nativity scene graces The Globe's entrance lobby in December 1953. *Author's collection.*

By the 1970s, presents, angels, and ribbons had replaced the Nativity scene. *Author's collection.*

> *Just like your home, The Globe gets all dressed up for the coming holiday season. Did you realize that? We cleaned every nook and corner of our store; we're putting up our bright and glistening holiday decorations. We're getting ready for our holiday guests. Our shelves are stocked with gift assortments of every description—we've something for Mom and Dad, Sis and Brother, Grand-parents* [sic]*—Uncles—Aunts—you name them—we've got it! Our holiday windows have been the "talk of the town" for many years, thanks to the terrific ideas of Jim Hines and his associates. Our bakers have made delicious fruit cakes—cookies—holiday stolen and boy, have we made candy, tons of it.*
>
> *Can the diets! It's holiday time. Let's eat, drink, and be merry! Be "merry" to each of your customers—because we have believed for 91 years that a gift from The Globe means more. Be "merry" to each of your customers because it is through their "buying at The Globe" we, too, can have a "Merry Christmas." Don't neglect to say "Merry Christmas" to your customers—it is our personal wish to them but we need you to convey the message for us. Our humble wish to you—may your days be bright and may all your Christmas dreams come true. Santa Claus will arrive Nov. 22nd.*[179]

In grand fashion, Santa Claus arrived at The Globe in late November of each year. Leaving the sleigh and reindeer at the North Pole, the jolly old elf instead utilized a helicopter specially commissioned by The Globe to fly him to Scranton. Upon arrival, he would land on the rooftop deck of the Easy Park garage where he would be greeted by store and city officials as well as a throng of excited children and their parents. From there, he would enter the store and make his way to The Globe's Fantasyland of Toys.

From 1980 to 1989, Santa's home at The Globe was called "Santa's World." Organized by the Junior League of Scranton, it was the apex of the store's Christmas décor. Santa's World could be reached by ascending an open staircase to the fifth floor where customers would find a sparkling holiday wonderland. Upon arrival, children were greeted with a series of rooms that centered on holiday and popular themes such as teddy bear villages, candy lands, gingerbread houses and even the Land of Oz. Themes also often centered on popular children's programming of the day such as the Smurfs, the Jetsons, the Care Bears and the Flintstones. One popular attraction at Santa's World was the post office where a direct phone line linked the store to the North Pole so that children could phone in their holiday wishes and where they could mail their letters to Santa. Special

Above: The Globe's Santa Claus parade, circa 1982. *From the Mark Boock Collection. Courtesy of Greg Boock.*

Opposite: A full-page advertisement shows area residents the many goods and services available on each floor of The Globe during the holidays. Note Santa Claus at the top of the "Santa Stairs" on the fifth floor. *Author's collection.*

"Santa-Gram" stationery was made available so children could write their letters directly from Toyland. The children would later receive a mailed reply from Santa with a reminder in the letterhead that The Globe was his "headquarters." Another attraction was the Santa's Secret Shop—a kid-sized store with kid-sized prices where area children could buy gifts for their parents and loved ones for one dollar and below. As parents were not allowed in the shop, Globe staff members assisted children in choosing and purchasing presents.

At the end of their journey through Santa's World, children arrived at Santa's magical castle, where, seated on a gold and velvet throne, the big man in red greeted his young visitors with rosy cheeks and a warm smile. Placed on Santa's knee, some children froze due to numbing shyness, while others reacted with giggles, squeals and a seemingly endless list of

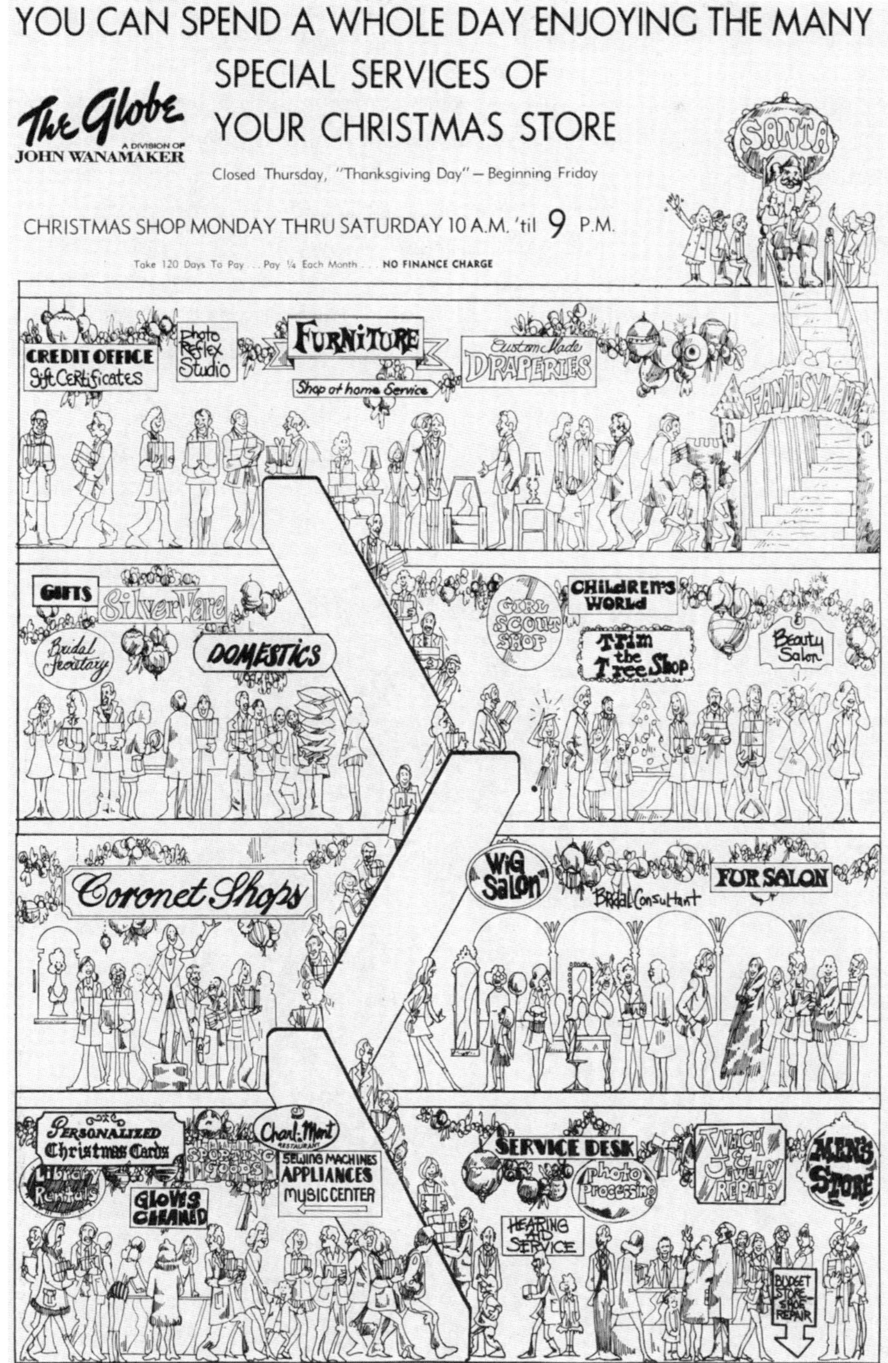
YOU CAN SPEND A WHOLE DAY ENJOYING THE MANY
SPECIAL SERVICES OF
YOUR CHRISTMAS STORE
The Globe
A DIVISION OF
JOHN WANAMAKER
Closed Thursday, "Thanksgiving Day"—Beginning Friday
CHRISTMAS SHOP MONDAY THRU SATURDAY 10 A.M. 'til 9 P.M.
Take 120 Days To Pay . . . Pay ¼ Each Month . . . NO FINANCE CHARGE
SANTA
CREDIT OFFICE
Gift Certificates
Photo Reflex Studio
FURNITURE
Shop at home Service
Custom Made
DRAPERIES
FANTASYLAND
GIFTS
SilverWare
Bridal Secretary
DOMESTICS
GIRL SCOUT SHOP
CHILDREN'S WORLD
Trim the Tree Shop
Beauty Salon
Coronet Shops
WIG Salon
FUR SALON
Bridal Consultant
PERSONALIZED
Christmas Cards
Library Rentals
SPORTING GOODS
GLOVES CLEANED
Charl-Mont
RESTAURANT
SEWING MACHINES
APPLIANCES
MUSIC CENTER
SERVICE DESK
Photo Processing
HEARING AID SERVICE
WATCH & JEWELRY REPAIR
MEN'S STORE
BUDGET STORE—SHOE REPAIR

requests. Still others reacted with abject terror, which was often humorously reflected in the photographs that were taken to commemorate the event. At the conclusion of their meeting with Santa, children were given a pin with his likeness and the phrase "Meet me at The Globe." The pin often included a jingle bell suspended from a red ribbon. Alternatively, children would often receive a Santa-themed coloring book as a souvenir of their trip. In addition to Santa's World, children had another opportunity to speak with Mr. Claus at the Charl-Mont's annual "Breakfast with Santa." Also attending the breakfast was The Globe's own clown character, Globo, which, like Santa himself, either elicited squeals of delight or screams of terror from the young crowd.

In 1986, The Globe's parent company, John Wanamaker, created its own holiday character to be sold as a stuffed animal along with a line of accessories and merchandise associated with it. During the 1980s, many department stores hurriedly cashed in on the teddy bear craze by creating their own

With the help of "Daffodil," the author summoned the courage to speak with Santa Claus at The Globe in 1989. *Author's collection.*

line of Christmas characters. Hence, one could find furry holiday friends in places such as Pomeroy's in Wilkes-Barre and Reading, which peddled "Pom Pom Pomeroy"—a hound dog dressed in holiday hat and scarf. In Allentown, children could bring home Hess's V.I.P.—Very Important Panda. Across the nation, legendary retailing names sold characters such as Famous Barr's "Famous Bear," Marshall Field's "Mistletoe Bear," Abraham & Straus's "Abearham & Straus the Mouse," Rich's "Richie Bear" and Higbee's "Twigbee Bear." At Philadelphia's Wanamaker's store, officials settled on a simple plump polar bear dressed in a knit red sweater with green reindeer. The matching hat bore the bear's name—Rudi. Accompanying Rudi was a small storybook that described his adventure in meeting Santa Claus and becoming his helper. Wanamaker's heavily advertised Rudi Bear in print advertising and catalogues showcasing the bear and all of accessories one could purchase for him. These included different outfits as a clown, Hawaiian shirt, doctor, ballerina, hooded sweatshirt and bandana. Rudi-themed merchandise was also available and included bedsheets, slippers, cups, plates, cookie jars, placemats, candles, nightshirts, aprons, sweatshirts and a host of other items. Rudi was even made part of John Wanamaker's iconic Christmas light show, where he remains to this day.

When Rudi premiered at The Globe in Scranton, he caused a local sensation. While successful in all of Wanamaker's locations, Rudi proved to be exceptionally popular in Northeastern Pennsylvania. The bear was so popular that it warranted producing other characters that were exclusive to The Globe. Thus, 1987 saw the introduction of Snowflake, a long-haired white sheepdog with a hat like Rudi's, and Little Huggy Bear, Rudi's "little brother" who wore a green hat and scarf with red reindeer. The gimmick with Little Huggy Bear was that it could be turned inside out and become a red satin Christmas present with green ribbon. As part of the promotion, a storybook and cassette tape were produced that featured all three characters. In 1988, Little Huggy Bear was replaced by Daffodil, or "Daffy" for short. Daffy was a pig who, reflecting her counterparts, bore a red knit scarf with green reindeer. In addition to these characters, The Globe also had giant-sized Rudi Bears produced that were given out as contest prizes to area children and organizations. Long after the store's demise, the characters remain as popular as ever and still grace many homes in Northeastern Pennsylvania during the holiday season.

Rudi, Snowflake and Daffodil were also made into costumes worn by performers in the store's annual Christmas parade to welcome Santa Claus to the city. Featuring floats, fire engines, high school bands, balloons and

MEET RUDI'S B

SNOW

YOU CAN BUY RUDI OR SNOWBALL FOR

*You can get either RUDI, your favorite playful little bear cub or SNOWBALL, a shaggy playful white puppy that is RUDI's best friend for only $12 each, when you purchase $50 or more worth of Globe merchandise in any one day. Have your receipts validated in our two Shops On One and Four.

. . . AND YOU CAN BUY LITTLE HUGGY BEAR, RUDI'S BROTHER FOR JUST 9.95

IN OUR BEARSPOT SHOPS ON ONE AND FOUR!

A 1987 advertisement for Rudi Bear and his friends, Snowball and Little Huggy Bear. *Author's collection.*

Top: Rudi Bear, Little Huggy Bear, Snowball and Daffodil. *Author's collection.*

Bottom: Tibby arrives at The Globe accompanied by Mickey Mouse and Globe Store officials. *Courtesy of the Lackawanna Historical Society.*

Reactions varied during the author's visits with Tibby and Freckles in the late 1980s. *Author's collection.*

various characters, including Mickey Mouse, Mother Goose, Darth Vader and Tony the Tiger, the parade was a store tradition that was later taken up by the Scranton Jaycees after The Globe closed. After Santa ceased using a helicopter to travel, he was whisked to Scranton on board a special train that stopped at the Lackawanna Station on Lackawanna Avenue. From there, he would join the parade, which would proceed down Spruce Street and up Wyoming to The Globe's front doors, where he would receive a jubilant welcome.

Although Christmas was the biggest holiday in The Globe's calendar year, it did not ignore other special days and events. The best example of this was Easter. As spring approached, The Globe's candy department created chocolate bunnies and special candy to fill empty Easter baskets. Upstairs, a portion of the fifth floor was transformed into Bunnyland, where the Easter Bunny would reside for the season. The Globe had two Easter bunnies: Tibby and his country cousin, Freckles. Tibby was dressed in a fancy purple outfit with gold braiding, pink shirt with lace, yellow collar and white gloves. Freckles, on the other hand, was a bit more informal in his denim overalls, flannel shirt, red bandana neck scarf and straw hat. His name came from the multitude of freckles that dotted both cheeks of his face. Like Santa, Tibby and Freckles were welcomed to the city in their own parade that saw them arrive on a train at the Lackawanna Station. They then proceeded down Lackawanna and Wyoming Avenues to The Globe, where they greeted cheering crowds and were welcomed by store and city officials. For Bunnyland, Santa's throne doubled as the Easter Bunny's chair so area children could sit on the rabbit's knee and have their picture taken. When visiting either Tibby or Freckles, children were given a pair of cardboard or paper bunny ears that bore The Globe's script logo.

In addition to Christmas and Easter, The Globe observed other holidays with special sales for Mother's Day, Father's Day, Columbus Day and Washington's Birthday. Valentine's Day received special attention from the store's candymakers and florist. Halloween was celebrated by inviting area children to a party in the store's fifth-floor Community Room for a day of ghoulish fun that included pumpkin contests, special treats, clowns and toys. Before attending, kids were encouraged to browse the wide array of costumes available for purchase.

The Dry: Scranton's Gift Center

Like The Globe, the Dry went to great lengths to welcome the holidays to Scranton. At Christmastime, the store draped its façade with fancy decorations, including garland, wreaths and trees. In its early years, a cloak of pine covered each of the entrance marquees with letters declaring the Dry as "Scranton's Gift Center." In the windows, shoppers were told to "look to Scranton Dry Goods Co. for Christmas savings!" In the 1950s, giant bells were placed above the entrance marquees to signal the coming of Christmas. These were replaced over the years with lighted snowflakes and giant candles as the Dry's decorating scheme evolved. The lighted decorations were not only beautiful in and of themselves, but they also highlighted the intricate details of the store's neoclassical façade at night.

As the holiday display windows were synonymous with the downtown Christmas shopping experience, the Dry spent lavishly each year creating new and entertaining scenes in its ten windows. Originating from the visual display workshop on the eighth floor, a room cluttered with colorful swags of cloth, branches, fake trees, paint cans, bows, ribbons and props, the Dry's display team conjured up holiday magic as they planned the next year's decorating theme. Led by Steve Komora, the planning stage began in June of each year.[180] Once an idea or theme had been selected, the team worked to build the decorations that would grace the sales floors and display windows the following November. Komora considered the windows to be a stage, and as such, lighting was just as important as the actual mechanicals and props that stood within them. Komora stated that "with proper lighting, you can do an awful lot."[181] He went on to say that "we buy colored tubes of pink, yellow, green, and blue. By using the green and yellow we get a good shade of blue. When pink is mixed with blue, we get purple. The lights can give you a crazy effect."[182] Combining new and elaborate displays with effective lighting created an entertaining yuletide show each year at the corner of Lackawanna and Wyoming Avenues. While the store did not mind spending lavishly on these decorations, the cost had to be justified. At the height of the dance craze of the 1960s, for example, the Dry spent $8,000 on a life-size Mr. and Mrs. Santa Claus that performed the Twist. After their initial use in the windows, they were recycled and reused throughout the store for several Christmas seasons to balance out their exorbitant price tag. As *Sesame Street* became popular, the Dry invested in a life-size holiday display featuring

A 1930s view of the Dry at Christmastime. *Author's collection.*

The most important gifts of all . . .

This is a check list of gifts that may escape your attention . . . a reminder of things to give to people you may not know . . . a suggestion of items priceless in value that will cost you nothing.

THE GIFT of brotherhood to those discriminated against.

THE GIFT of blood to those wounded in freedom's cause in far-off lands.

THE GIFT of comfort to those in distress.

THE GIFT of moderation in speech and good example in conduct.

THE GIFT of a friendly greeting to strangers.

THE GIFT of patience and forebearance to those who may disagree with you.

THE GIFT of good citizenship to your community.

THE GIFT of understanding and happy homelife to your children.

THE GIFT of wholehearted response to your duties as a family member, a worshipper at a church or synagogue, an employee or employer, and as a citizen of this free country.

THE GIFT of daily thanks to the Source from Whom all gifts flow.

These are the gifts you may find while shopping in our store. But they will be found at no counter, you will find them only in your own heart.

MERRY CHRISTMAS AND HAPPY NEW YEAR TO ALL

CLOSED TOMORROW, CHRISTMAS

SHOP WEDNESDAY AND THURSDAY 10 TO 9

Opposite: Every holiday season, the Scranton Dry would publish a list in local papers reminding shoppers that the most important gifts could not be found in any store. *Author's collection.*

This page, top: The Dry at Christmastime during the 1960s. *Author's collection.*

Middle: The chimney from which Santa and Mrs. Claus appeared each season. *Author's collection.*

Bottom: Scranton Dry Goods Christmas window. *Author's collection.*

characters from the show, including Big Bird, Cookie Monster and Oscar the Grouch. Despite their cost, the windows generated huge excitement for the store and drew people through the doors.

One of the holiday traditions at the Dry was a contest asking local female participants aged thirteen to nineteen to create a doll using a kit that could be purchased at the store for twenty-five cents. At the conclusion of the contest, store judges, including Ike Oppenheim's widow, Constance, would choose the winning entries. Winners were eligible to win different prizes that included trips to Europe and New York City, a piano, a portable TV set, luggage and other smaller prizes. After being displayed in the store for a time, the dolls were then given as Christmas gifts to underprivileged children throughout the area.

For those whose dolls needed repair, the Dry set up a "doll hospital" each holiday season where young people could bring their favorite companions to the "chief surgeon," Ethel Hollister Cumming.[183] The Doll Hospital's existence preceded that of the Dry's and initially started in the J.D. Williams store on North Washington Avenue. Ike Oppenheim kept the tradition going when he invited Cumming to open the hospital in his new store. When the Dry moved to Lackawanna and Wyoming Avenues in 1917, Cumming and the doll hospital followed it. The doll hospital proved to be a popular feature of the store's toy department each year and was another example of the Dry's dedication to its customers, particularly its youngest ones.

The Dry's most cherished holiday tradition was one that was not intended to generate any profits for the store whatsoever. After the hustle and bustle of last-minute shoppers had ceased on Christmas Eve, Oppenheim family members and other store officials gathered toys, coats, clothing and candy and personally loaded them onto the store's delivery trucks. From there, the goodies were trucked all over the area to be distributed to less fortunate children who otherwise might not have anything under the tree on Christmas morning. Founded by Ike Oppenheim on the store's first Christmas Eve in 1912, this tradition was a continuing testament to the caring and generous nature of the family behind the Dry's success.

To welcome Santa Claus to the city, the Dry employed its Wyoming Avenue marquee to hold a giant red brick chimney. At the start of the holiday shopping season, anxious crowds gathered below the marquee to watch store and city officials welcome Mr. and Mrs. Claus as they emerged from the chimney. Often, the mayor of Scranton would be on hand to present Santa with the key to the city as hundreds of screaming children looked on in delight. After waving to the adoring throng of people, Santa then made his way to his throne in the Dry's toy department on the sixth floor. Later, the toy department moved to the fourth floor and so did the Dry's Santa. In Toyland, children were able to speak with Santa Claus, have their picture taken and receive a special gift in the form of a pin or coloring book. Not to be outdone by The Globe, the Dry also hosted a breakfast with Santa in its Tea Room. Dubbed the Mistletoe Breakfast, the event featured special guests such as the "Christmas Princess" or Miss Judy from *Hatchy Milatchy*, a popular local children's television program.

At Easter, the Easter Bunny received the same royal treatment as Santa at the Dry. As the holiday approached, the Wyoming Avenue marquee was again used, but this time it held a giant Easter Egg. On the date of their arrival, Mr. and Mrs. Easter Bunny broke out of the giant egg to delight

A 1964 advertisement inviting area children to the see the Easter Bunny and Uncle Ted of local television fame at the Scranton Dry. *Author's collection.*

the same crowds and dignitaries that had welcomed their Christmas counterparts. As research suggests, Mrs. Easter Bunny was only seen for this event. Mr. Easter Bunny, on the other hand, then took his place in Bunnyland in the Dry's toy department, where he could meet with area children. The bunny also gave out special gifts such as activity booklets and bunny masks. In the late 1970s, the Dry acquired a giant mechanized rabbit that could speak and interact with children from his special house on the second floor. With print advertising boasting "the talkingest [*sic*] Easter Bunny is at Oppenheim's," the new chatty bunny clearly set the Dry apart from The Globe's friendly but silent Tibby and Freckles.

Hard work, creativity, generosity, goodwill and fierce but friendly competition led The Globe and the Dry to create fun and fanciful holiday traditions that wowed the young and young at heart. Long after the two stores were no more, the memory of these traditions lives on in the minds and hearts of those fortunate enough to experience them. As they were during their heyday, the holidays are perhaps the most powerful force in sustaining the stores' existence in the consciousness of their former customers.

6

THE TEN COMMANDMENTS OF GOOD BUSINESS

When walking into a department store during the twentieth century, one was met with an army of polite, courteous and knowledgeable staff members who catered to the customer's every want and need. A sales associate was never difficult to find or unwilling to be of assistance. This standard of excellence was expected of each associate of The Globe and the Dry and was reinforced through training, rewards and a culture of respect and pride in one's work.

One of the familiar sounds associated with The Globe, the Dry and other department stores of the era was that of the call chimes that sounded frequently on all sales floors. Part of the background noise of nearly all upscale stores, the "bing-bing" sound of the bells was employed to page managers, security and other associates. When hired or promoted, the employee was given a specific code or sequence of chimes that would signal to them on the sales floor that they were to call or report to the central offices or a specific department. For example, a manager may receive a code of two bells, a pause, one bell, a pause and four bells, or 2-1-4. Thus, as they went about their work on the sales floor, they always had to keep an ear out for their code, 2-1-4. Considered more subtle and less disturbing to customers than making announcements on the public address system, the chimes added to the air of sophistication that upscale department stores strived for.

When one was hired as an associate at The Globe and the Dry, whether as a salesclerk or as a member of upper management, they were held to very high standards at all times, both in manner and in appearance. In those days,

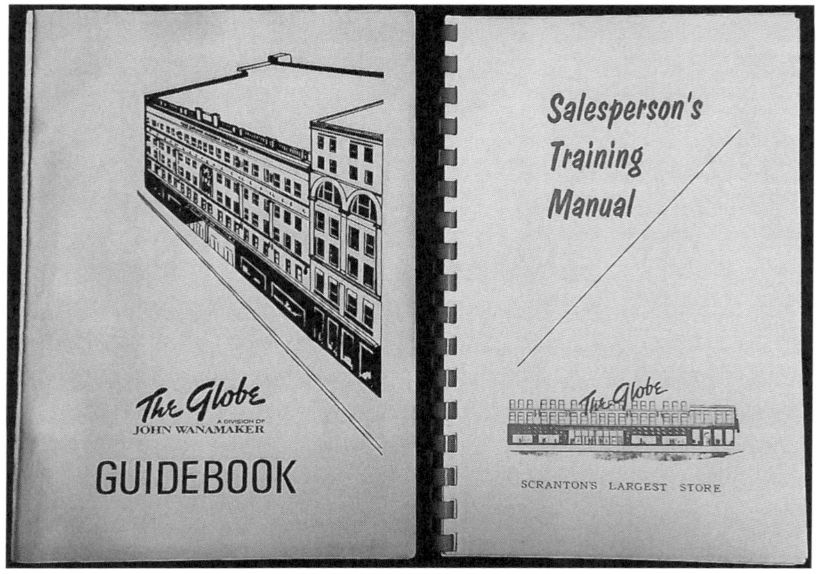

Salesperson's training manuals from The Globe. *Author's collection.*

it was completely unacceptable for a representative of a fine department store to be seen on the sales floor in casual clothing. Therefore, formal attire was required to always be worn by associates. Female associates were expected to dress conservatively in a dress or blouse with a skirt of moderate length, stockings and appropriate, formal footwear. Often, stores required their female employees to adhere to a color that was most associated with the store itself. Female associates of Fowler, Dick and Walker–The Boston Store of Wilkes-Barre, Pennsylvania, for example, were instructed to wear dresses in dark gray or navy blue, while those working in Pomeroy's across town were to wear brown. Male associates were to report to work each day in a full suit, dress shirt, tie and shined dress shoes. Hair, fingernails and general appearance were also to be neat, trim and presentable to the public. This strict policy of dress and appearance was nonnegotiable, even under the most extreme circumstances. When President Jimmy Carter issued an edict that all public buildings were to reduce their use of air-conditioning during the summer of 1979, The Globe and the Dry, by then known as Oppenheim's, did not relax their dress code policy as temperatures soared inside the two stores.[184] Men dressed in full suits were not even allowed to remove their jackets if they were dealing with the public. As representatives of the store, the associates understood that formality and proper appearance were a must despite their discomfort. The Globe's management explained the reasoning behind this strict dress code by telling associates that "since you reflect the store, make your impression a total one. Be sure you are clean and attractively dressed with becoming make-up and hair-do [*sic*] and that your manners are as pleasant as the more tangible garments you wear in public. YOU ARE THE GLOBE."[185]

In addition to looks, an associate's demeanor could mean the difference between a sale and an offended customer. The client's needs came first, and as the saying goes, "The customer is always right." Hence, associates were never to argue with a patron, no matter how quarrelsome they became. Training dictated that friendly and helpful employees create a welcoming environment that warmly invited customers to visit time and again. To reinforce this rule, The Globe released "The Ten Commandments of Good Business" to its associates in June 1974. A customer-centered set of guiding principles, the bulletin stated the following:

I. A customer is the most important person in any business.
II. A customer is not dependent on us. We are dependent on him.
III. A customer is not an interruption of our work. He is the purpose of it.
IV. A customer does us a favor when he calls. We are not doing him a favor by serving him.
V. A customer is part of our business, not an outsider.
VI. A customer is not a cold statistic. He is a flesh and blood human being with feelings and emotions like our own.
VII. A customer is not someone to argue or match wits with.
VIII. A customer is a person who brings us his wants. It is our job to fill those wants.
IX. A customer is deserving of the most courteous and attentive treatment we can give him.
X. A customer is the life-blood of this and every other business.[186]

One of the most important aspects of being an associate at The Globe and the Dry was their knowledge of the store and of their individual departments. Moreover, many employees were required to know how to perform several functions of salesmanship throughout the store, including how to handle cash and credit sales, help prevent shoplifting, taking inventory and running the stores' NCR Model 53 mechanical cash registers. In earlier years, a vast network of pneumatic tubes was used to transport payments, sales slips, change and receipts to and from a central cash office in lieu of having registers at each sales desk. It was imperative that this multitasking on the part of staff looked effortless so that the customer had confidence in the associate waiting on them and in the store itself. Thus, employees were required to be well-versed in all their duties. To this end, both The Globe and the Dry had extensive training materials and programs to make certain that their employees had all the necessary skills to provide superb customer service.

When a sales associate became proficient in their job duties, they then had to learn the wants, needs and idiosyncrasies of the clientele they would be serving. Buying patterns on the part of the customers were mentally noted and memorized by many salesclerks so that when they returned, the clerk knew what the customer desired before they ever uttered a word. As one perfected their expertise in terms of their knowledge of the goods they sold and the departments they ran, the associate was respected as a professional and seen as an authority figure by the buying public. If a woman was undecided in the shade of lipstick that she should purchase, for example, the attending associate was able to offer educated suggestions based on the available inventory and their experience as authorities in beauty. This service, professionalism and expertise earned the staff the undying loyalty of their customers.

Those who worked behind the scenes were just as knowledgeable in their duties. When freight trains delivered car after car of new stock from New York and Chicago, stock room workers, truck drivers, maintenance workers and a host of others conducted a well-choreographed routine to ensure that merchandise was quickly unloaded from the trucks, processed and distributed to the appropriate buyers and department managers. The Globe's loading, receiving and marking departments were in the first, basement and sub-basement levels of the Easy Park structure. At the Dry, stock was received at the rear of the building in large truckloads and then lifted via freight elevators to the eighth-floor processing center. There, it was checked, marked and sent to the seventh floor, where the store's buyers would select their stock each morning. The large spiral chute extending from the eighth floor to the basement served to feed merchandise to the appropriate floor managers. Occasionally, merchandise would lodge itself in the chute and store employees would either throw a large crate of soap down to dislodge it or repel down a rope to clear the chute manually. In addition to those dealing with merchandise, the stores employed a team of craftsmen, electricians, painters, maintenance workers and repair workers to keep the facilities always looking and functioning at their best. Though customers rarely interacted with them, the stores' legion of behind-the-scenes workers kept these beehives of retail buzzing at a steady pace.

If a shopper wished to make a purchase but did not want to venture downtown, The Globe and the Dry offered an amenity that allowed them to shop from the comfort of their home: the personal shopper. The

Behind-the-scenes views of The Globe Store's offices and staff members. *Author's collection.*

service centered on the idea that the customer could select what they wished to buy from a newspaper advertisement, store catalogue or prior knowledge of the store's inventory and "phone in" their order to the personal shopper. It was she who traversed the sales floors to fulfill the customer's order. Then, the order would be packaged and quickly loaded on one of the store's delivery trucks for delivery. If one was calling The Globe's personal shopper, they would dial **DI**amond 4-7271 and ask for Miss Jane Barry. At the Dry, the customer would call **DI**amond 2-3281 and ask for Miss Sue Martin. If the customer preferred, they could simply send a filled order form and preferred payment method to the store care of Miss Barry or Miss Martin. Both stores claimed to the public that they employed only one personal shopper who would tend to all their customers. This, of course, was impossible. Instead, The Globe and the Dry employed a team of personal shoppers who all went by the alias associated with their store. According to Max Hess Jr., the purpose of this little white lie was to create a personal connection with each customer.[187] That is, the client would call "their" personal shopper frequently and address them as either "Jane" or "Sue" as if she were a good friend.

To keep associates abreast of the goings-on in their store, The Globe and the Dry frequently distributed bulletins, updates and, in the case of The Globe, an in-house employee publication. When one received their pay envelope from the Dry, they would find their cash wages, their paystub and one or more employee bulletins. For example, one note to associates of the Dry asked them to take their lunches in the employee cafeteria upstairs if they found that the Tea Room was becoming busy. The Globe's method of distributing information to its staff was a bit more creative. In the 1960s, the store developed an in-house employee magazine known as the *Globe Trotter*, which was distributed to the staff once or twice a month. The *Trotter* included articles on important events, funny stories, jokes, directives, advice, salutes and in-store news such as weddings, births, promotions and retirements. The "Let's Talk It Over" column instructed or reminded employees of store policy and procedures. The magazine proved to be highly successful and helped improve information flow, lift employee morale and make one proud to be an associate of The Globe Store.

We appreciate your co-operative spirit and loyalty to the store during the year, and particularly during this Holiday Season, which is always a trying time for everybody.

We hope we can remain together during the year 1939, and through our combined efforts make it a happy and successful one for all of us.

Wishing you and your family a Merry Christmas and a Happy New Year.

Sincerely yours,

SCRANTON DRY GOODS COMPANY

President

Opposite: A *Globe Trotter* employee magazine from June 1969. *Author's collection.*

This page, top: Globe and Scranton Dry/Oppenheim's service pins. *Author's collection.*

Bottom: A 1938 holiday message from I.E. Oppenheim to his employees. *Author's collection.*

In return for their dedicated service, both stores took pains to make their associates feel appreciated. Publications such as the *Globe Trotter* detailed associates' length of service, major accomplishments, awards or a simple acknowledgement of a retiring staff member or new face joining the store. In addition to these publications, employees were honored at store-sponsored dinners at which they were grouped together based on their years of service. Hence, one would find tables that seated the "10 Year Club," the "20 Year Club" and the "25 Year Club." At the dinner, a special ceremony was held to induct new members. Part of the induction included the presentation of a commemorative pin that reflected one's years of service. Depending on the number of years, jewels and pearls were often imbedded in the pin as a token of the store's appreciation and respect.

In addition to the service dinners, store-sponsored contests and getaways were other methods the companies used to show their gratitude to their staff. The Dry, for example, would sponsor a summertime picnic at Hilcrest, the Oppenheim family's estate, in LaPlume. At these events, swimming, games, refreshments, meals and camaraderie were the order of the day. These

Left: Globe associates pose for a photo during one of the store's employee picnics. *Author's collection.*

Opposite: A Globe Store softball jersey. *Author's collection.*

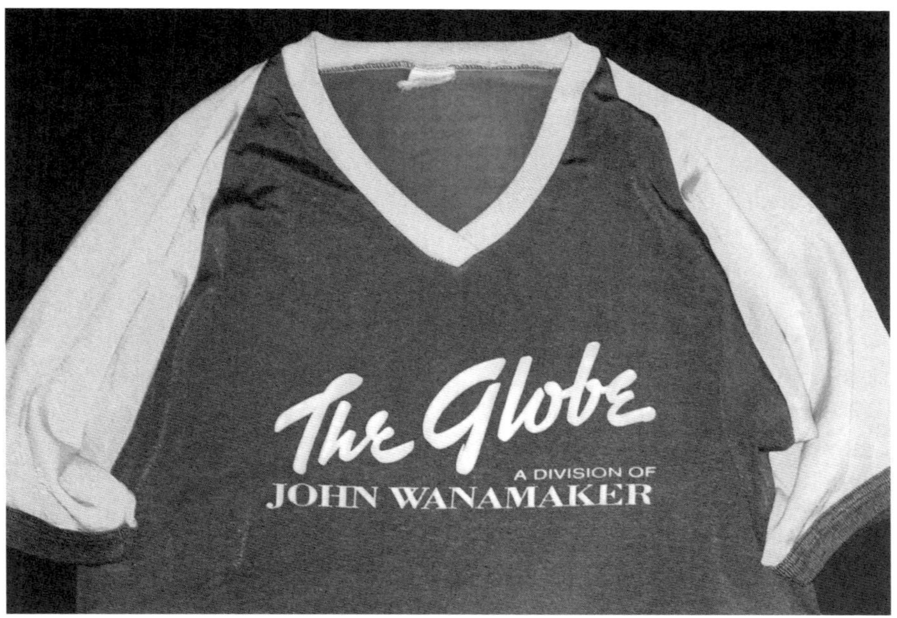

efforts paid big dividends, as the retention rate of employees was extremely high. In 1968, this fact was evident at the Dry when a large group of veteran employees was allowed to be the first to ride the store's new set of street floor escalators. All of them had been with the firm when it installed the first set of moving stairs in 1924.[188]

To build camaraderie among staff members and a sense of teamwork, The Globe and the Dry, along with many other Scranton-area businesses, fielded sports teams that would compete with one another in what was known as the Industrial League. Softball, basketball and bowling were among the sports played. Team practice was held after hours or on breaks. At the Dry, the employee recreation area on the eighth-floor rooftop often served as a softball practice field. A veteran employee, Rupert "Mike" Bowen, once recounted that many impromptu Dry ballgames were held on the roof set against the city's skyline.[189] The fun continued until a foul ball usually ended the match. Official games and tournaments between the businesses' teams were held at local fields and bowling alleys. Afterward, the teams' scores were published in the sports sections of local papers. In addition to in-house employee teams, The Globe, along with several other local stores, sponsored Little League teams for area children as part of their effort to support the community.

While they are remembered fondly, it is important to note that not all the stores' extracurricular activities were associated with sports. The arts were also given considerable attention. The Globe's staff members, for example, maintained a talented glee club for a time. The Globe Store Glee Club performed at various charitable functions, benefits and dances.

Personal touches involving customer service were everything at The Globe and the Dry. Going a little further for one's clients resulted in immense appreciation for and loyalty to the store. When the birth of a baby was announced locally, the Dry was sure to send a card to the proud parents congratulating them and to remind them that the store had a full infant's department to meet their every need. These little touches undoubtedly helped build a strong personal connection between the store and the customer. This "friendship" is sorely missed by many decades after the stores closed for good.

7
FASHION FLOOR

In decades past, American society often dictated that one dress in their best if they ventured out in public. Regardless of their socioeconomic status, people were expected to dress in business attire to shop, attend religious services, go to parties, participate in social functions and work if they held any type of white-collar job. Inasmuch as the bulk of a department store's customer base consisted of female shoppers, retailers devoted entire floors of their emporiums to women's fashions. Often, they aptly called them "fashion floors." The Globe and the Dry both maintained extensive fashion floors to serve their customers. The stores' buyers traveled to major cities and across the "globe" to bring the latest styles to Scranton. With The Globe's located on the second floor and the Dry's located on the third, both stores vied to be Scranton's fashion leader.

According to Max Hess Jr., age and income level are irrelevant when it comes to caring about and improving one's appearance.[190] During the department store golden age, most women looked to their local department stores for the latest fashion trends in clothes, shoes, hats and accessories. Therefore, they carried clothes to cater to everyone's needs, usually at three or four price levels.[191] The highest price level consisted of expensive luxury goods that retailers understood would probably not move quickly.[192] Their purpose, Hess states, was to create an aura of sophistication, quality and good taste.[193] Women who could ill-afford these high-priced fashions were drawn through the doors by the store's high-class, fashion-conscious reputation and, in turn, purchased the more moderately priced clothing that made up the lion's share of the department's takings.

Stores often set aside large areas or rooms on the sales floor to devote to their most exclusive inventory such as Hess's French Room in downtown Allentown. At The Globe, the store's top-level merchandise was grouped into the "Coronet Shops" on the second floor. The Coronet departments were select areas of the store's fashion floor that sold fine dresses, coats, shoes, accessories and "foundations"—that is, women's lingerie. Labeling the most expensive goods with the Coronet title was intended to clearly denote to the customer that this was the best and latest fashion that The Globe could offer. For dresses, the department did include a more affordable option called "Coronet Moderate Priced Dresses" for those seeking value along with the prestige that came with the Coronet label. In addition to the Coronet Shops, The Globe maintained a separate "Designer's Salon," which sold high-end clothing from new and upcoming designers as well as those that were established but still on the cutting edge of fashion. Over at the Dry, shoppers would find the latest, most exclusive merchandise in the store's "Chandelier Room." Named for the glittering crystal light fixtures that were gracefully suspended from the ceiling, the department was the Dry's equivalent to The Globe's Coronet Shops and Hess's French Room.

Mid-priced items were sold under the "Better" label. Departments bearing this moniker included "Better Dresses," "Better Coats" and "Better Shoes." These items were still considered chic and trendy, but they were also more affordable for the middle-class shopper, who most often patronized the store. Both The Globe and the Dry used the word *better* for the more moderately priced merchandise. It was this price point that often generated the most traffic and profits for the entire department.

Below the "Better" price level was the stores' lowest price point, which at The Globe was housed in its "Budget Shops." An extension of the basement Budget Store, the Budget shops, which included "Budget Dresses," "Budget Coats" and "Budget Shoes," catered to the bargain hunter looking for quality merchandise at the lowest possible price. Often, these departments were located on the street floor, where impulse buys were most likely to take place. Not unlike The Globe, the Dry extended its budget-priced "Pin Money" concept to women's fashions on the third floor, where it also attracted the budget-minded shopper. As was the case with the price point directly above it, the low-priced apparel in the Budget Shops and Pin Money departments did much to generate profits for the fashion departments at both stores.

In addition to the three main price levels that The Globe and the Dry offered, the fashion floors maintained several other departments that sold more specific soft lines of merchandise. Ladies looking for fine furs would be greeted by a full-service fur salon at both stores. The Dry, the first store in the area to install cold storage vaults on the premises, offered customers the opportunity to safely store their investments in a climate-controlled environment when not in use. Another vital part of the stores' fashion floors was the Bridal Salon, staffed with an army of knowledgeable saleswomen. There the bride-to-be could find all she needed to fulfill her dreams of the perfect day, including wedding dresses, bridesmaid's dresses and veils. To promote this, The Globe and the Dry invested heavily in materials that were designed to help the customer keep track of needed products and completed purchases as her wedding day approached. They also served as a sort of

Left: A 1971 advertisement for The Globe's remodeled second-floor Coronet Designer's Salon. *Author's collection.*

Right: A 1963 advertisement for the Scranton Dry's Chandelier Room on the Third Floor of Fashion. *Author's collection.*

The Globe's newly remodeled second floor of fashion in 1971. *Author's collection.*

journal that preserved one's memories of the entire experience. Another service pioneered by the stores' salons was the "bridal registry." Here, a couple could create a list of their wants and needs with the advice and assistance of a professional bridal consultant. Later, the list would be made available to friends and loved ones to use as a reference when shopping for wedding gifts.

To ensure that these fine fashions properly fit women of all body types, both The Globe and the Dry maintained fully staffed alterations departments where, for a nominal fee, women could have any garment altered, reshaped or have gussets added so to achieve that perfect look. The alterations team at the Dry was led by a Miss Yevich, who, according to Susan Oppenheim Dimond, was "a genius when it came to making a purchase fit properly."[194] Ellis Oppenheim Jr. states that alterations departments were vitally important to department stores' fashion floors, particularly for designer fashions, better-priced clothing, bridalwear and formalwear, as they "did not make clothing to fit all body types such as petites, shorter women, and plus sizes for women over a size 14."[195] Tall sizes were also difficult to find off the rack in the designer, bridal and better priced salons, so they often had to be altered as well.

To show off these fashions, both stores hosted live fashion shows for the community. Employing local women as models, the shows were intended to create excitement for the stores and the new incoming styles being offered for the next season. Local venues such as Scranton's majestic Masonic Temple as well as the stores themselves served as the sites where crowds would gather to see their neighbors strut down the runway wearing the trendiest clothes. Occasionally, the stores would invite special guests to their fashion shows. In 1962, for example, the Dry hosted actor, singer and teen idol Fabian at one of its shows along with that year's Miss Pennsylvania. Aside from all the glamour, the shows served a practical purpose for the stores' customers. Prior to the advent of the internet, local women depended on the professional expertise of the stores' buyers and the other staff members who organized the shows to learn what new styles the world was wearing.

Younger women and girls were not forgotten at The Globe and the Dry. Both stores offered the latest in teen-oriented apparel situated in their own themed departments. At The Globe, the Young Miss Globe shop catered to teenage girls while the Dry did the same with its Young Miss Scranton shop. In addition to its Young Miss Globe shop, The Globe's Justeen Shop offered the latest teen fashion trends. The Pizazz Shop, the Dry's answer to the Justeen Shop, also offered trendy clothes for young female shoppers. In the 1970s, the Dry even featured a department that was devoted entirely to Girl Scouts. It is worth noting that this department posed an interesting form of competition from the Dry, as its archrival across the street had been named as the Girl Scouts' official headquarters in the city.

The stores were extremely aware that young people were their customer base of the future. As such, both The Globe and the Dry were eager to build loyalty with this age group by hosting special events such as live teen fashion shows and in-store finishing, or "charm," schools. Here, area girls were taught good manners, good taste and good behavior. The Globe's Seventeen Beauty Workshop, for example, was a seven-week course where local students aged thirteen to sixteen received lessons in fashion, modeling, manners and good grooming. Although dated by today's standards, the schools proved to be popular and helped build a strong relationship and trust between the store and its future customers.

In addition to the schools and workshops, The Globe and the Dry hosted teen fashion boards that performed a variety of functions at the stores. The Globe's College Board consisted of girls who were chosen during a selection process that went from Easter to the beginning of June. During the month of August, members would work in various departments that tended to college

students, thereby learning the preferences and needs of their peers. The experience culminated in a gala fashion show held at the nearby Masonic Temple. Those who were not selected during the application process had the opportunity to serve as models and ushers at the show. The College Board was designed to promote The Globe's "Back to College" sales event

A Scranton Dry Goods Company fashion window. *Author's collection.*

and was very successful each year. At the Dry, its fashion board was open to all local high school girls who were interested in fashion and wanted to serve their community. If one's application was under consideration, she was invited to the store for an in-person interview. If selected, the young woman would join twelve to fourteen other girls who would meet monthly at the store. Their purpose was primarily to act as liaisons between the store and their peers in the surrounding area. Additionally, they were to act as representatives of the store at various social and charitable functions. In keeping with the Dry's community spirit, the board would select a charitable cause to support each year. Throughout the year that they served, board members were expected to participate in various store functions such as the Dry's annual Back to School Fashion Show. They were also expected to actively participate in the charitable functions they had elected to support at the beginning of their membership.

The fashion floors at The Globe and the Dry were the go-to places for many of Scranton's well-heeled as well as its more modestly heeled female customers. Regardless of their background, every woman was made to feel welcome as soon as they stepped off the escalator or through the elevator doors. Department staff made every effort to make the women feel good about themselves and their appearance. A place of beauty and sophistication, the fashion floor strongly reinforced the stores' image as places of high quality, high style and good taste.

8

A TREE GROWS IN SCRANTON

In decades past, giving back to the communities that made them successful was widely recognized as part of a department store's civic duty. Charitable contributions to the cities in which they did business not only benefited the townspeople; they also benefited the stores themselves as their efforts generated an incalculable amount of goodwill and loyalty from customers. The Globe and the Dry understood this well and took great pride in giving back to the people of Scranton and the surrounding area.

The Globe: Keeping Northeastern Pennsylvania Beautiful

The Globe was a leader in civic and charitable causes in Scranton. It conducted countless efforts to better Northeastern Pennsylvania and the people who lived there. One of its most famous efforts was its annual tradition of giving away pine tree saplings to local schoolchildren on Arbor Day. The Globe's attention to nature and the environment was imbued into it by its founders. An early example of this was the large greenhouse and conservatory that was donated to the city's Nay Aug Park by store founder John Cleland. Decades after his passing, the store faithfully continued

Cleland's legacy of community service and love of nature. As Arbor Day approached each year, The Globe purchased thousands of Norway spruce pine seedlings from local nurseries in preparation for the holiday. After the plants were delivered to the store, Globe associates inspected and processed each tree, which was then loaded into the company's fleet of delivery trucks. From there, the seedlings were distributed to all the local school districts throughout the area. The districts would subsequently give each child ranging from kindergarten through eighth grade a seedling to take home and plant in their yard. In the end, nearly fifty thousand seedlings were distributed each year. In 1978, on the occasion of The Globe's one hundredth anniversary, the one millionth tree was given out. It was the hope of the store's management that this effort would aid in the beautification of the surrounding area and educate area children on the importance of protecting the environment. Begun in 1961 under the direction of The Globe's visual director, James Hines, the event quickly became a warmly regarded tradition and something that local students looked forward to each year. It also succeeded in helping raise awareness of the meaning of Arbor Day and the importance of nature in everyday life.

In addition to the Arbor Day tradition of giving away pine seedlings, The Globe reached out to the surrounding area through several other means. One was its "Globe Athlete of the Week" program. With the first held in the early 1950s, the Globe Athlete of the Week became a weekly program sponsored by The Globe and the *Scranton Times* in which area high-school athletes were recognized for their achievements. Every Sunday, the student athletes were interviewed during a radio show on local radio station WQAN. The interview, which was later moved to local station WEJL, was then broadcast across Northeastern Pennsylvania. In addition, all the student-athletes and their coaches were treated to a formal dinner at the Charl-Mont Restaurant in May of each year.

As The Globe possessed an enormous amount of room—250,000 square feet spread over six floors and a basement—it often lent some of this space as well as its good name to local service organizations and charities. For example, the store's third floor became the local headquarters for Scranton's official Girl Scout Shop. To promote this special department, The Globe held an annual "Cookie Day" to increase the sale of Girl Scout cookies. Boxes of the sweet treats could be purchased at one of several stands positioned throughout the building. In 1971, Cookie Day enabled the Scouts to sell over 1,100 boxes of the delicious treats at the store alone.[196] The Globe was also concerned about the health and well-being

A 1978 advertisement for The Globe's annual Arbor Day distribution of pine seedlings to local elementary school students. *Author's collection.*

of its associates and customers. In 1970, the store hosted the Lackawanna County Tuberculosis Association, which conducted free diabetes checks for all Globe Store customers and associates.[197] In this event, almost four hundred people were tested. Other special nonprofit events sponsored by or assisted by The Globe included the Scranton Philharmonic Youth Concerts, Little League teams, charm schools, Teen Fashion Boards and the public showing of the most current educational films of the day. These are but a few examples of The Globe's civic-mindedness and caring attitude toward the people who worked and shopped there.

The Dry: Faith, Family and Community

The Dry also firmly believed in giving back to the people of Scranton and the surrounding communities. In addition to its annual tradition of giving away toys, clothes and candy on Christmas Eve and its holding teen boards that stressed the importance of charity and community service, the Dry Goods team worked tirelessly to make Northeastern Pennsylvania a better place to live through a host of other charitable events, sponsorships and educational seminars. Like The Globe, one way the Dry accomplished this goal was to open its huge store facilities to local charitable and service organizations. The Lion's Club, for example, made use of the store's sixth floor cafeteria annually for its Educational Week for the Blind. In 1970, the Dry, in cooperation with the Auxiliary of the Pennsylvania Association for the Blind, held live fashion shows and displayed designed aids and appliances used by blind people in observance of Helen Keller Day.[198] As the family was very passionate about the issue, Ike Oppenheim and his family personally funded several programs to help the blind as well. In addition to helping the blind, the store's focus on its customers' health and well-being was exemplified in its countless workshops, displays and educational conferences that focused on the subject. This was manifest in the numerous blood drives in cooperation with the American Red Cross, free cancer screenings and a host of other health-focused events that were held at the Dry over the years. The Oppenheim family regularly donated the store windows to promote local health and charitable functions at a time when a store's display windows were thought to be directly linked to its profits. In 1965, Scranton Dry Goods Company Vice-President Ellis M. Oppenheim served as the chairman and leader for the fundraising drive to build the city's state-of-the-art Community Medical

In 1977, Oppenheim's "saluted" colleges and universities by holding weeklong events showcasing each institution's offerings. In this advertisement, Oppenheim's salutes the University of Scranton. *Author's collection.*

Center on Mulberry Street. He also actively participated in the planning and building stages of the hospital.

In addition to the health of its customers, the Dry and the Oppenheim family were devoted to causes that furthered education in Northeastern Pennsylvania. This was proven time and again by the store and the family. At Keystone Junior College in LaPlume, for example, Ellis Oppenheim served as a trustee. Jane Oppenheim, Ellis's sister-in-law and wife of Richard, also actively served at Keystone as a board member, benefactor and trustee. In 2004, Jane was instrumental in the construction of the Oppenheim Family Children's Center on Keystone's campus, which provides early childhood education to preschool-age children as well as serving as a training ground for students majoring in education and related fields. In addition to Keystone, many other educational institutions throughout the area have greatly benefited from the generosity of the Oppenheim store and family. The University of Scranton, which was going through a period of great expansion in the 1950s and 1960s, received several large financial gifts from the Oppenheim Foundation for the construction of new classroom buildings. In 1958, the Dry donated an elevator to the Scranton School Board for use in its facilities.[199] In a 1977 show of goodwill to many local institutions for higher education, the Dry conducted week-long celebrations that saluted each area college or university. Heavily promoted in newspaper advertisements, the salutes included displays, guest speakers and demonstrations that all promoted the strengths and offerings of the institution being celebrated that week.

The local arts were not forgotten by the Oppenheim family. In 2015, the Oppenheim Center for the Arts opened at the United Neighborhood Centers in Scranton. It houses a stage, a pottery room and studio space for recording, dance, and photography. Jane Oppenheim, who served on the board of the United Neighborhood Centers, helped cut the ribbon at the center's opening ceremonies. In addition, Jane also served on the board of the city's Everhart Museum.

The Dry's and the Oppenheim family's fervent desire to help others made both paragons of charity and community service in Northeastern Pennsylvania. Family and store patriarch Ike Oppenheim set the pace in terms of this continuing spirit of compassion and generosity. It is perhaps his greatest legacy to his family and the community that he called home. One of his most lasting contributions is the establishment of the Oppenheim Foundation, which is a family-run organization that regularly donates funds and services to local charitable and educational causes. Ike was also largely responsible for the creation of the United Way in Lackawanna and Wayne Counties. Later, both of his sons would go on to serve as its general chairmen. Ike and *Scranton Times* editor and publisher E.J. Lynett helped found the Community Welfare Association, later the Scranton-Dunmore Community Chest and forerunner to the United Way. Both men co-chaired the drive in 1942. Ike served as its president from 1928 to 1929 and chairman of the budget committee prior to that.

Ike's compassion stretched far beyond the city limits. He actively participated in the collection of funds to aid political refugees suffering in Poland and to help reconstruct the Jewish homeland in Palestine.[200] He also was active in efforts to aid Jews in Germany and eastern Europe suffering under the brutality of Adolf Hitler's Nazi regime during World War II. In addition to his work to help those suffering overseas, Ike was extremely involved in many local charitable, civic and religious organizations. One such organization was the Amos Lodge, B'nai B'rith, where he served on the board of directors.

A man of strong faith, Ike Oppenheim was committed to local Jewish faith and community groups. For many years, he served on the board of directors of the Young Men's Hebrew Association (YMHA) in Scranton. At the end of his tenure in 1946, he was honored by the organization for his service. During his years on the board, Ike served as chairman of the board for the YMHA's Jewish Community Center, or JCC, from 1928 to 1946. Before his chairmanship, Ike had served as vice chairman of the board for several years. After his tenure, he continued to serve as an honorary member. In 1954, Ike's eldest son, Ellis, joined a group of other prominent local citizens to spearhead the construction of a new, ultramodern facility for the Scranton JCC, which continues to see to the health and wellness of people of all backgrounds throughout the surrounding area. After Ike's death in 1954, the Oppenheim family honored his memory by donating the Oppenheim Chapel to the city's Temple Hesed. Along with the chapel, the Oppenheim Institute was established at the temple, which invites scholars, leaders, authors and others to speak on a variety of issues.

Ike Oppenheim's descendants continued his legacy of service in countless ways. His oldest son, Ellis, in addition to those service roles previously discussed, is credited with many selfless contributions to his community. Some of these roles include his service as general chairman of the campaign to raise $1 million to build Temple Hesed's new building on Lake Scranton Road, as board member of the Madison Avenue Temple and as an active member of the Scranton JCC and B'nai

B'rith.[201] Ellis also served as a member and president of the Scranton Chamber of Commerce, the Commercial Association of Scranton and the Scranton-Lackawanna Development Corporation, where he also chaired the executive committee. In 1954, he chaired the United Jewish Appeal and served as president of the Boys Club of America. Ellis's wife, Esther, was also active in numerous service and civic organizations, including the Junior League of Scranton.

Ike's younger son, Richard, followed his father's and brother's example and led a life of service to his community. During World War II, Richard served his country with the Thirty-Seventh Division Medical Corps.[202] For his wartime service, Richard was awarded with the Philippine Liberation Medal, the Philippine Republic Presidential Unit Citation Badge and the Purple Heart. After Ike's death in 1954, Richard assumed the supervisory role of the Dry's Christmas Eve tradition of distributing toys and clothes to needy children until the store closed. After the store's closure in 1980, the tradition became known as the Christmas Bureau, for which Richard continued to serve as a volunteer and interviewer. Like his brother, he was a member of the Scranton Chamber of Commerce's board. He also served on the board of directors at Temple Hesed, the Scranton-Lackawanna Jewish Federation and the Scranton-Lackawanna Industrial Building Company, or SLIBCO. Moreover, Richard's service included his volunteer work for SCORE and Meals on Wheels. Richard's wife, Jane, was dedicated to community service locally and nationally for her entire life. Her contributions are immeasurable and include service on many boards, including Hunter College, United Neighborhood Centers, Junior League, Voluntary Action Center, CMC/Geisinger, Scranton Area Foundation, Temple Hesed, Union for Reform Judaism, Women for Reform Judaism and the World Union for Judaism.[203]

The Oppenheim family's philanthropic efforts are well-known, and it has been rightly recognized for them. Various members of the family have been honored for their lives of service by the countless organizations that they have served. Constance Oppenheim, Ike's widow, was recognized by the University of Scranton in 1964 when she became that institution's first Jewish woman to be awarded an honorary doctorate. Her daughter-in-law Jane received the same honor in 2004. Jane's impressive list of honors and awards includes the Junior League of Scranton's Margaret L. Richards Award for Outstanding Contributions to the Community, the Martha Wollerton Award for the Greatest Contribution to the Overall Welfare of the Community, the Hunter College Hall of Fame for Outstanding

Community Service, the Jewish Community Center's Woman of the Year Award and the B'nai B'rith Americanism Award. In 2015, Jane was named a Distinguished Daughter of Pennsylvania. Ellis Oppenheim received a considerable number of awards during his life of service, including the Boys Club of America Distinguished Service Award in 1955 and the Americanism Award for Amos Lodge 136, B'nai B'rith in 1963 for meritorious civic and community service.

The Dry itself was also recognized throughout its existence for its outstanding reputation of service to the community. In August 1971, the store was honored with the Bonnie Bell Community Service Award for its Teen Board's tutoring program for migrant children.[204] The store had provided on-site classroom space for the tutors from the Teen Board and their students to meet once a week for the entire winter season. The Dry also held Halloween and Christmas parties so the tutors could become acquainted with the children. Countless other well-deserved awards were bestowed on the Dry and the Oppenheim family for their innate drive to serve Scranton and its people.

9

GROWING BRANCHES

As the 1960s progressed, it became increasingly clear that the future of retailing lay in the suburbs. Once bustling downtown emporiums became neglected and deserted as their owners and former customers shifted their focus to strip malls and enclosed shopping centers. When the first enclosed shopping mall opened in the 1950s and Levittown, Pennsylvania, became a national symbol of modern living, the concept of the suburban shopping center began creeping ever closer to Scranton. The Globe and the Dry responded with parking garages, renovations and more modern methods of merchandising. Despite this, the management at both stores realized that to stay competitive, they would have to grow and expand beyond the downtown or risk being crushed under the weight of their newly arrived rivals.

The Globe: On the Wings of an Eagle

The Globe acted decisively. In 1955, the Cleland-Simpson Company reached a deal with Wilkes-Barre businessman Julius Long Stern to purchase the venerable Isaac Long department store in the city's downtown. Presiding over the Diamond City's Public Square, the stately store had served the Wyoming Valley since 1873.[205] The store's namesake and founder, Isaac Long, was a cousin to Jonas Long and his sons, whose lives in local retail were relatively short-lived in comparison to Isaac's. The grand Victorian structure Isaac Long had occupied since 1891, the Welles Building, was known locally as the first in the valley to feature an elevator. Although it was smaller than its rivals at twenty-five thousand square feet, Isaac Long and its 190-member sales force maintained a reputation for consistent excellence and quiet elegance that attracted the area's carriage trade. One example of Isaac Long's sterling reputation was its signature pink and gray gift boxes, which eventually became status symbols in and of themselves. As Wilkes-Barre's answer to specialty stores in larger cities such as Bergdorf Goodman, Bonwit Teller, Saks Fifth Avenue and I. Magnin, Isaac Long made the most of its three sales floors by filling them with expensive fashions, fine china and silverware, high-end gifts, jewelry and accessories.

In October 1956, the Cleland-Simpson Company invested over $100,000 in revamping and updating the aging store. The interior received extensive remodeling, expansion and a new, more efficient layout. The street floor received many cosmetic improvements, including mirrored columns, wider aisles and a pleasant soft green color scheme. New elevators were installed that ran to all five floors of the building, and the store was completely air-conditioned. Additionally, merchandise offices that were formerly located on the Second Floor of Fashion were moved to the fourth, doubling the fashion floor's selling space and allowing for the addition of several new departments. Like the street floor below, the second floor received a new look with shell-pink walls, burnt-orange accents and turquoise wall-to-wall carpeting. Modern fixtures and rebuilt departments were installed on the third floor to create a complete home center that included china, silverware, bedding, toiletries, linens, draperies and gifts. To keep up with the growing popularity of driving downtown, an enclosed bridge was installed that connected the store's second floor to the third level of the Miners National Bank Parkade located directly behind the building. These updates gave Isaac Long's a feeling of brightness, spaciousness, convenience and modernity. Isaac Long was further freshened and updated in May 1963. As part of the modernization effort, a fresh coat of bright white paint was applied to the façade to give it a cleaner look.[206] The exterior also received new, modern display windows, entrances and a new sign. The interior was extensively modernized as well. With a relatively modest $3 million in annual sales, Long's was never a big moneymaker for the Cleland-Simpson Company. Nevertheless, the store was still a shrewd purchase for The Globe, as it gave the company direct access to the bustling Wyoming Valley market. Moreover, Isaac Long, with its high-class reputation, instantly became a glimmering, exquisite jewel in the Cleland-Simpson Company's crown.

JULIUS LONG STERN

ELLEN V. STERN

"Because none of our children wishes to dedicate his life to operating the Isaac Long Store, we have sold it.

We are certain that the Globe Store of Scranton is the ideal purchaser from every standpoint. Their organization has an excellent history of accepting civic responsibilities. Their employee relationships are outstanding. They have a long record of excellent merchants in tune with Isaac Long traditions and policies.

We want it known that we did not negotiate with other prospective purchasers. Our respect for the Globe Store management, our love for Isaac Long and our gratitude to our employees were the reasons we went to the Globe and offered our business for sale.

We feel that our policies and traditions, our place in the community and the security of our employees are safe in the capable hands of the Globe Store management."

Signed by . . .

Julius Long Stern
Ellen V. Stern

JOHN A. NOBLE

"The Isaac Long Store is a good store with a history of sound management. Its position in Wilkes-Barre retailing is excellent. Its reputation among customers is outstanding. It has a pleasant personal relationship with its customers. It has many of America's most respected lines of goods. Isaac Long is in every way a good store. All these things have come about because of the abilities of the people who form the Isaac Long organization and because of the close adherence to Isaac Long policies.

We contemplate no change in policy.

We contemplate only these changes in personnel—Carl [illegible], has been promoted to store manager. Dean Humpherys has been promoted to Merchandise Manager.

Isaac Long is a good store—we feel it's our primary responsibility to keep it that."

Signed by . . .

John A. Noble

What the Purchase of Isaac Long's by Scranton's Globe Store Means to You

There is an Even Greater Isaac Long in Your Future.

The belief in quality . . . bringing together the finest names in American merchandise here in Wilkes-Barre's fine store, has made Isaac Long unique in its position. Its uncompromising belief in the good things of life includes plans to bring more and more of these good things to you: expanded service, greater shopping convenience and many other improvements.

The purchase of Isaac Long's by Scranton's Globe Store is the most natural thing in the world. The two stores think alike and operate by the same high merchandising standards. Now, by working together, they will make possible an even greater Isaac Long in your future.

Isaac Long

A 1955 Isaac Long advertisement assuring customers that the quality and service the store was long known for would be continued and even enhanced under the Cleland-Simpson Company's stewardship. *Author's collection.*

By the late 1960s, The Globe's growing sales volume, the addition of the Isaac Long store, and its extensive delivery area throughout Northeastern Pennsylvania made it clear to Cleland-Simpson Company management that larger and more efficient warehousing operations were required. The old warehouse on Spruce Street was housed in a small, outdated building that could no longer accommodate the needs of this growing department store empire. Thus, in 1967, Globe Store president John A. Noble announced that the firm had acquired a 14.2-acre tract of land for $45,000 along Rocky Glen Road in nearby Moosic for the construction of a new warehouse. Built at a cost of $1 million, The Globe's new 85,000-square-foot warehouse and distribution center opened in 1968. The one-story building consisted of masonry and steel covered in an insulated metal sheathing that gave the warehouse a sleek and modern look. When it opened, the new warehouse was described as "a modern design, one-story structure which will centralize warehousing and delivery of furniture, floor covering, mattresses, television sets and major appliances, in addition to a wide variety of miscellaneous bulk merchandise."[207] While the sprawling complex could comfortably meet all The Globe's warehousing needs, it also served as its new distribution center. The expansive loading dock could handle four tractor trailers loading and unloading merchandise simultaneously as well as the store's own fleet of fourteen delivery vehicles. Continuing a tradition started at the old Spruce Street warehouse, The Globe regularly held "Warehouse Sales" where large items such as furniture or major appliances could be purchased at reduced prices directly from the warehouse. This helped move large and expensive merchandise that could not always be displayed in the limited available space at the downtown store.

The year 1968 proved to be a pivotal one in The Globe's long and storied history. With the opening of the modern warehouse in Moosic, its $15 million in annual sales and its extremely loyal customer base, The Globe's reputation as one of Scranton's leading department stores had caught the attention of several nationally recognized Philadelphia merchants. John Wanamaker and Lit Brothers had both served the City of Brotherly Love for generations, and both were eager to expand into the Northeastern Pennsylvania market.[208] Although both maintained a formidable presence in their home city, the two retail giants had very different philosophies of conducting business. While Wanamaker's was patrician and traditional, Lit Brothers, or "Lits," merchandised its stores for more budget-minded customers. Its hulking Center City Philadelphia

An artistic rendering of The Globe's modern distribution center in nearby Moosic, Pennsylvania. *Author's collection.*

store consisted of a string of cast iron–fronted buildings that had been cobbled together over the years until Lits covered an entire city block. Both Wanamaker's and Lits believed that they could make their retail formula work in Scranton and Wilkes-Barre. Accordingly, the two retail giants placed competing bids on the Cleland-Simpson Company.[209] Although both formulas were successful, the winning store had the potential to take The Globe in a different direction than the one that Scrantonians were accustomed to.

Wanamaker's won. On August 21, 1968, the John Wanamaker Company of Philadelphia purchased the Cleland-Simpson Company and its two stores, The Globe Store and Isaac Long, for an undisclosed sum. Recognizing that The Globe's formula worked in Scranton, the powers that be at Wanamaker's wisely chose to keep the store's name and management team intact. John A. Noble was retained as president of both The Globe and Isaac Long and the Cleland-Simpson Company's complement of 875 associates kept their jobs. While Wanamaker's purchased the businesses, they did not purchase the real estate holdings of the Cleland-Simpson Company. The Globe's landmark downtown building, Easy Park Garage and Moosic Warehouse would be retained by the Simpson Real Estate Corporation, a separate company controlled by the heirs of John Simpson. Wanamaker's agreed to lease these facilities to continue the retail operation. While Scranton's famous store was left more or less unchanged by the Wanamaker deal, all its advertising, credit plates, boxes, bags and other items bearing the store's logo would now say "The Globe—A division of John Wanamaker."

John Wanamaker, both the man and his store, were legends in Philadelphia. Founded as a men's and boys' clothing store by Wanamaker and his brother-in-law, Nathan Brown, on April 8, 1861, the store was first known as Oak Hall–Wanamaker & Brown.[210] Brown died in 1868. Despite the loss of his business partner, Wanamaker continued to expand the business and opened a second store in the city the following year.[211] In 1876, Wanamaker moved his growing enterprise into a converted Pennsylvania Railroad freight depot he renamed the "Grand Depot."[212] Located along the city's bustling Market Street, Wanamaker's did enormous business. By the early 1900s, even Wanamaker's aging Grand Depot could no longer safely accommodate the business and needed to be replaced. To address this, he commissioned noted Chicago architect Daniel Burnham to design a new store that could match Wanamaker's lofty dreams.[213] Burnham was no stranger to retail design. Some of his other works include Marshall Field's in Chicago, Filene's in Boston and Gimbels on New York City's Herald Square. The result was a monumental twelve-story structure containing over one million square feet of floor space.[214] Completed in 1911, its seven-story Grand Court was the centerpiece of the new store and contained one of the largest pipe organs in the world to entertain customers. It also housed a 2,500-pound bronze eagle.[215] Both were originally created for the 1904 St. Louis World's Fair, and their presence made them symbols of the store. The eagle became a favorite meeting place for Philadelphians, and the phrase "meet me at the eagle" was commonly uttered by those venturing into Center City.

John Wanamaker's massive Philadelphia flagship was famous for its impressive Grand Court, which was home to the store's pipe organ and bronze eagle, the latter being a favorite meeting place for many Philadelphians. *Author's collection.*

Largely responsible for the department store model that became the standard in the retailing world,

In a not-so-subtle ad, the Dry congratulated John Wanamaker on its purchase of The Globe Store while simultaneously pointing out that it was now Scranton's only locally owned department store. *From the* Scranton Times, *August 21, 1968. Author's collection.*

John Wanamaker had many firsts to his credit. He was among the first merchants to place so much faith in the power of consistent and creative advertising. In addition to this, his store was the first to install electric lights, the first to have a telephone, the first to have a pneumatic tube network system and the first to hold a "White Sale." As a deeply religious man who was unwavering in his faith in Christian values, Wanamaker believed that everyone should be equal before God. Therefore, everyone should pay the same prices and store associates should not engage customers in haggling. As a result of this policy, which was first instituted in October 1871, Wanamaker invented what would become the most basic and common of retail tools: the price tag. Wanamaker's also implemented the first return policy in a store, known as a "money-back guarantee."[216]

John Wanamaker's religious convictions also made him one of the best bosses as he deeply believed in treating his associates with kindness and respect. His store offered employees several luxuries and conveniences as well as good pay and generous benefits. Wanamaker's combination of innovation, ambition, respect and kindness made the store a huge success and served as part of his legacy. The company continued to abide by the convictions of its founder, which enabled it to expand outside of Philadelphia. Wanamaker himself oversaw the firm's expansion to New York City with another enormous flagship store (formerly A.T. Stewart & Company) in 1896. His successors continued to spread the Wanamaker name and reputation after his death in 1922 with suburban locations in New York, New Jersey, Pennsylvania and Delaware. Inasmuch as these traits closely matched those of the Cleland-Simpson Company, Wanamaker's was an excellent match for The Globe.

The Dry: Discover Oppenheim's

As The Globe explored new horizons, the Dry also began looking to expand beyond the city limits. On April 2, 1965, members of the Oppenheim family, along with local dignitaries and hundreds of well-wishers and customers, cut the ribbon to open the new Scranton Dry Country Store in suburban Clarks Summit. Located on the corner of State Street and Main Avenue in the middle of the village's quaint business district, the store featured "apparel and accessories for suburban living" as well as the "Boytique Shop" for boys.[217] Reflecting the taste of the time, the interior décor was of Early American design carried out in red brick and red cedar with period furnishings and fixtures. The theme was extended to the exterior façade, which featured red brick, dark brown panels, large display windows and a large bronze eagle that soared above the store's sign that was done in gold Colonial font. The firm of Edinger Wyckoff Inc. designed and decorated the store to be chic, comfortable and fashionable and still blend in to its small-town, rural surroundings. Compared to its massive, eight-story counterpart in downtown Scranton, the Country Store was

An advertisement celebrating the grand opening of the Dry's new Country Store in Clarks Summit. *Author's collection.*

discover
Grand Opening tomorrow, 10:30 A.M.
Register to win prizes!
Prizes to be awarded every day in every department.
GRAND PRIZE: $1000 Oppenheim's Shopping Spree
Plus . . . over $5000 in additional merchandise.
Here are just a few of the many prizes to be awarded in every department:
• G.E. Porta-Color 10" TV, $199 value.
• King Koil Spinal Guard Mattress and Box Spring Set, 291.90 value.
• F & M Mediterranean Lounge Chair, 129.95 value.
• Farberware Stainless Steel Cookware Set, 29.99 value.
• Lee's 9' x 12' unbound carpet, No. 4767, choice of 6 colors, 119.88 value.
• Decorator Industries Custom Bedspread, 119.95 value.
• Holabird Drop-Leaf Maple Table, 99.95 value.
• Springmaid Pinsonic full-size bedspreads, 32.99 value.
• Krebs Stengel Governor Winthrop Desk, $95 value.
• Franciscan 20-piece Starter Set, $58 value.
• Nova Crystal Table Lamp, $75 value.
• Spring-Air Health Center Mattress and Box Spring Set, 179.90 value.
• Seth Thomas Wall Clock, $80 value.
• Centura 20-piece Starter Set, $58 value.
• Women's Russ Togs Blazer-shell-pants set, $58 value.
. . . plus many, many more prizes . . . come in and register.
november 21st

An award-winning 1974 advertisement that heralded the opening of Oppenheim's new store at the Pocono Village Mall in Mount Pocono, Pennsylvania. *Author's collection.*

relatively small at only five thousand square feet spread over one floor. Nevertheless, the Scranton Dry Country Store proved to be an immediate hit among local shoppers and represented the Dry's first foray into the suburbs.

Encouraged by the success of the Country Store, the Oppenheim family began preparations for a much larger expansion project that would see the Dry enter the scenic Pocono Mountains. In 1973, store officials entered a contract with the newly constructed Pocono Village Mall to build a full-line forty-thousand-square-foot anchor store. Construction began shortly after. Located at the busy intersection of PA Routes 611 and 940 in Mount Pocono, Pennsylvania, the mall held much promise in becoming a major shopping center. As the Poconos had long been served by the venerable A.B. Wyckoff Department Store in downtown Stroudsburg, the area was thought to be prime for another major department store to enter the growing market. When announcing the new store to the local press, Dry Goods Secretary-Treasurer Richard Oppenheim stressed that the company's community-minded spirit would be extended to the Poconos when he said, "We like to be good neighbors."[218]

Throughout the design and building phases of the Mount Pocono project, the Oppenheims spared no expense in making the new store a showplace of modern retail design. Built and furnished at a cost of $1 million, the firm of Gilboy, Stauffer, Giombetti, Skibinski and Davies of Chinchilla, Pennsylvania, served as consulting architects while Oliver Associates of New York City carried out the interior design. Like the Clarks Summit Country Store, designers sought to incorporate the store's surroundings when designing the interior and its furnishings. Natural woods, earth tones, lush carpeting and modern, subdued lighting fixtures created a relaxed, upmarket look that reflected the serene woods and rolling landscape of the Pocono Mountains. Upon entering the store, customers were greeted by a grand Palladian central court topped by a giant dome housing a bath boutique, cosmetics, perfumes, jewelry and accessories. The rest of the departments could be accessed from this central hub via large, wood-framed arches that gave the impression that the store was composed of small, intimate shops. Unlike the Clarks Summit operation, the Pocono Village Mall branch was a complete department store that featured many of the same departments that were found in the downtown Scranton store such as fashions for the family, appliances, furniture and home furnishings. It even featured a Santa Claus at Christmastime and its own teen board. The store layout, resembling pie wedges instead of the traditional grid format, was both unique and striking and represented the Dry Goods' best efforts in creating a totally new and beautiful anchor store. To promote it, full, multipage advertisements were taken out in local papers that showcased the unique sales floor and encouraged shoppers to "discover Oppenheim's." The advertisements were so creative and well-done that they were nominated for and eventually won a first-place award at the annual Interstate Advertising Managers meeting in 1974.

On November 21, 1974, a gala celebration heralded Oppenheim's arrival in the Poconos. Pocono Mountain High School band provided musical entertainment while store officials, representatives from the surrounding area, Mount Pocono Mayor Joseph Battisto and hundreds of customers crowded the five-hundred-space parking lot to witness the historic event. Rabbi Milton Richman asked the blessing before Ellis and Richard Oppenheim along with Mayor Joseph Battisto cut the ribbon opening the new store. With that, the main doors swung open, and the crowds jammed through the entrance lobby to view the newest and most modern retail store in Northeastern Pennsylvania. Rebranded as "Oppenheim's," the title reflected a monumental name-change that had occurred in 1972 to modernize the company's image and reflect its expansion beyond Scranton. The throngs of people initially signaled that the company had made the right move in locating in the Poconos. It was hoped that the new Oppenheim's store would help further modernize the store's image and cement the Dry's place among the growing number of suburban stores that were beginning to dominate retailing locally and nationwide.

10

GOING DOWN

As the onslaught of suburban malls and shopping centers wreaked havoc on urban retail throughout the 1960s and 1970s, downtown department stores began feeling the strain in earnest. Many of the country's largest and most well-known emporiums closed up shop in central cities, including Crowley's of Detroit, Lit Brothers of Philadelphia and Hochschild, Kohn & Company of Baltimore. Venerable giants like Hudson's, Gimbels and B. Altman clung to their flagship stores until the 1980s, when they too succumbed to changing shopping habits and the deterioration of America's cities. Other famous nameplates simply vanished in the whirlpool of mergers and corporate takeovers that rocked the department store industry during the "Decade of Greed."

It was in this environment that The Globe and the Dry found themselves while the city that they had called home for so long seemed to be looking at its best days in the rearview mirror. Scranton had built itself, figuratively and literally, on the anthracite coal that lay beneath its feet. Many Scrantonians and their counterparts in surrounding communities made their living deep underground in the network of mines or on the spider's web of railroad tracks that snaked throughout the region. It was this vast number of well-paying, blue-collar jobs that enabled the middle class to shop at The Globe and the Dry and afford the level of quality and service that the stores were known for. With the advent of more efficient fuel and heating sources such as oil, gas, electricity and nuclear power, coal was on the decline. On January 22, 1959, "King Coal" was officially overthrown and dispatched when miners in the River Slope Mine in Jenkins Township, Pennsylvania, were, in violation of state law, instructed by Knox Coal Company management to dig dangerously close to the Susquehanna riverbed. This caused the thinning roof to collapse, which turned the waterway into a swirling vortex that flooded the mines below and killed twelve men. Later known as the Knox Mine Disaster, the filmed imagery of railroad and mine cars swirling about like bathtub toys in what was a desperate three-day effort to mitigate the flooding became etched in the mind of the public. Many now saw mining as an outdated, corrupt and dangerous industry.

As King Coal aged, sickened and died, the railroad industry that depended on him was severely affected. Without massive amounts of coal to transport, the need for the trains that carried it was eliminated. Scranton was no longer a destination place. Hence, passenger railroad service, whose decline was hastened by the popularity and affordability of automobiles, began disappearing as well. This decline culminated in the Delaware, Lackawanna and Western Railroad's and later the Erie-Lackawanna Railroad's flagship "Phoebe Snow" service, an important symbol of train travel's luxury and prestige, ceasing operations in Scranton on November 28, 1966. The final passenger train left the city on January 5, 1970, and the grand railroad station that had majestically stood as Scranton's gateway was boarded up. The colorful stained-glass ceilings and soaring marble columns of its main lobby sat forlorn, vacant and vulnerable to vandals and the elements. Down Lackawanna Avenue, the once sumptuous Hotel Casey, host to countless celebrities, dignitaries, politicians and even a few presidents, grew into a seedy shadow of its former self before closing forever as the Casey Inn in July 1982. Downtown was dealt another blow when the silver screens of theaters like the Strand, Capitol, Center and Comerford went dark, leaving it without a major movie house. As the local economy declined, so did Scranton's population. Younger generations, finding it increasingly difficult to find the kind of employment that had sustained their ancestors comfortably, left the area to find opportunity elsewhere.

Despite Scranton's seemingly unstoppable downhill slide, The Globe and the Dry still managed to hold their own thanks to their fiercely loyal, albeit mostly older, customer base. Resistant to change, many local shoppers still preferred the convenience of shopping downtown. They still used public transport to reach the two stores, each having its own stop in front of the main entrance doors. The Globe's Wednesday Specials and the Dry's

Mighty Monday Values continued to draw crowds. Longtime customers made time to relax and socialize in the ladies' lounge, grab a bite to eat in the store restaurant or meet friends or family for a day of shopping. Significant changes would have to be made, however, if The Globe and the Dry were to remain relevant and attract younger shoppers.

The Globe: Shopworn

Those changes were slow in coming to The Globe. To the dismay of Globe management, the store's parent company, John Wanamaker, did not invest in it at the same level as the Cleland-Simpson Company.[219] In 1965, for example, store president John A. Noble announced the installation of a cutting-edge NCR electronic control system that centrally processed transaction data for the entire store as well as serving to manage merchandise reports and accounting records. At the time, it was the most comprehensive computer system installed in a store of The Globe's size, which earned it national attention in retail circles. After the 1968 sale, Wanamaker's capital spending in Scranton was starkly different. This is presumably because The Globe was not Wanamaker's focus—that is, it was a single-store division in a small declining city, not the company's flagship. Wanamaker's dedicated more attention and money into building newer mall stores and maintaining its landmark headquarters. Moreover, The Globe had long enjoyed being at the top of the food chain among local merchants, with its only major competition being the Dry. Thus, Wanamaker's opted not to devote large funds into updates and renovations. As a result, the store began to show its true age. Apart from the Fashion Floor, which received a complete makeover in 1971, The Globe's interior décor started looking old and worn in spots. This was not the fault of the store's management or staff. Wanamaker's had given The Globe a great deal of autonomy, but Philadelphia still had the final say on major expenditures.

The company suffered a major setback in late June 1972 when Hurricane Agnes swept through the Northeast. Several major cities in Eastern Pennsylvania and Southeastern New York State suffered incredible damage when on June 22, 1972, torrents of rainwater from the stalled storm caused the Susquehanna River to overflow its banks and levee systems. The surrounding areas were inundated. Downtown Wilkes-Barre was hit particularly hard by Agnes's fury. Floodwater swept through the city turning

The Globe's main entrance in 1974. *Author's collection.*

Public Square, which had been a scene of constant automobile traffic, into a lake traversable only by boat. Most of the downtown businesses were ruined, including Pomeroy's, Lazarus, Fowler, Dick and Walker–The Boston Store and Isaac Long. Unlike the others, however, Wanamaker's did not rebuild and reopen Long's after the flood. Two years later, the vacant, flood-ravaged Isaac Long store was razed and replaced by the ultramodern Bicentennial Building.

The Dry: New Look. New Name. Same Heart.

The Dry seemed to be a bit more proactive during this period than its rival. The reason for this was simple. The downtown Dry Goods store was its owners' top priority and focus, as it was the flagship of the company. In 1968, the Oppenheim family invested $500,000 in a major renovation project that saw the complete overhaul of all seven selling floors of the Scranton store. The street floor underwent the most dramatic transformation. Giant, sparkling brass and crystal chandeliers now hung from the street floor ceiling complementing the newly installed fluorescent lighting system. Aisles were widened, and several departments were either moved or consolidated for customer convenience. A much brighter, cleaner and uncluttered appearance now dominated the store. The centerpiece of the street floor was its new "Fashion Gazebo." Located near the center of the floor, the gazebo showcased new and expensive merchandise such as fine jewelry. It also would serve as the headquarters for guest speakers such as fashion designers, make-up artists and local dignitaries.

Upstairs, a new specialized department designed for the home chef was constructed on the sixth floor. At the time, Americans were developing more sophisticated tastes in cuisine thanks in no small part to the prevalence of international chefs, cookbooks and television cooking shows such as Julia Child's *The French Chef*. Finding the ingredients and utensils necessary to create these gourmet dishes was often difficult locally. Recognizing this, the Dry's management incorporated the "Country Kitchen" as a separate shop in the housewares department to meet that demand. Here, shoppers could find unusual or difficult to acquire cookware and accessories such as soufflé

A 1968 advertisement lauding The Dry's new street floor and escalators following a major renovation of the entire store in 1968. *From the* Scranton Times, *November 1968. Author's collection.*

dishes, woks, paella pans, fish poachers, asparagus steamers, butcher blocks and tin and copper ware. The shop was also used to host guest chefs who would demonstrate how to prepare exotic cuisine using the utensils available at the store.

In 1970, the Dry's Third Floor of Fashion received a thorough makeover. All the fashion departments were redesigned and redecorated according to the latest trends. The Bridal Salon received new décor tastefully done in blue, white and gold. Millinery, Junior World, Pin Money Dresses and the Chandelier Room were also redecorated. New and exciting fashion departments were added during this time, including the "Pizazz Shop" and the "Bouquet of Fashion." The Pizazz Shop carried Mod fashions and after-school wear popular among teenagers of the era. The Bouquet of Fashion was a designer shop that carried world-famous as well as up-and-coming designer brands. Deep pile, luxurious carpeting, subdued lighting, designer-inspired color schemes and soft background music added an atmosphere of quiet elegance. The discreet lighting system was designed to accentuate the actual colors of the fabrics and clothing on display. A sub-department of the Bouquet of Fashion was the "Exotic Shop," which dealt exclusively in international lines as well as unusual designs from home and abroad. Here, one could find fashions from the Far East, Europe and Hawaii shown in a meticulously crafted display unit that reflected the region from which they came.

One major renovation removed what was arguably the Dry's most famous feature: its ancient wooden escalators. Since 1924, the moving stairs had trundled thousands upon thousands of Scranton's shoppers without fail and were a familiar and beloved landmark in central city. Despite this, they were not in keeping with the Dry's modernization effort and would have to be replaced. Thus, sleek steel Westinghouse escalators were installed on floors one through four giving each a more modern appearance as well as providing a smoother and quieter ride for shoppers.

In addition to a new look, the Dry also received new blood at the helm as a new generation began to make its mark on the Scranton institution. Ellis Oppenheim's son Ellis M. Oppenheim Jr. became merchandise manager and a vice president at the store, affectionately known to store associates as "Mr. O." He continued in that role until 1970, when he moved to New York City, where he took a similar position at the famed Fifth Avenue retailer Bonwit Teller. During the 1970s, the Scranton Dry Goods Company merged with a well-known retail institution in the Wyoming Valley, Bergman's of Edwardsville. Founded on April 16, 1916, by Justin Bergman Sr. and his brother-in-law and business partner Charles Pfifferling Sr., the store initially opened in a three-story building at 40–42 South Main Street in downtown Wilkes-Barre. In 1938, Seymour Dimond joined the firm and later became a partner. Other partners subsequently joined the company, including Justin Bergman Jr., Charles Pfifferling Jr. and John Dimond. Eventually, John Dimond became the sole owner of the store. As the company's fortunes grew, so did its downtown store. A fourth floor was later added, and in 1949, the entire complex was extensively renovated and expanded with the addition of an adjoining three-story building at 38 South Main Street.

A decade later, Bergman's became the first department store in the area to close its downtown location entirely in favor of a brand-new twenty-six-thousand-square foot store at the Narrows Shopping Center in nearby Edwardsville. The new location, with its elegant and modern design, was immediately popular with local customers who enjoyed the convenience of its one-story layout, suburban location and acres of free parking. Bergman's, like all the major stores in the Wilkes-Barre area, was devastated by the Agnes Flood in 1972. Quickly bouncing back from disaster, Bergman's rebuilt its store and reopened to the public, eventually becoming part of the revamped West Side Mall in 1987. The

Bergman's Department Store at the Narrows Shopping Center in Edwardsville, Pennsylvania. *Author's collection.*

store continued serving the people of the Wyoming Valley until 1991, when the store closed for good. Bergman's president, John Dimond, married Ellis Oppenheim's daughter Susan in June 1971. As a member of the Oppenheim family and firm, Dimond took on several duties at the Scranton store as well as running his own store in Edwardsville. With the addition of this new generation, a renewed level of energy and excitement was brought to the Scranton Dry.

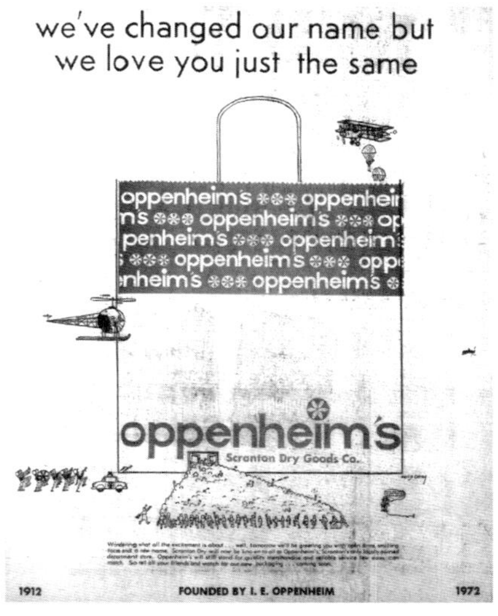

A 1972 advertisement celebrating the Scranton Dry's official name change to Oppenheim's. *Author's collection.*

The Dry's renewed energy and trendy, modern attitude was reflected in its 1972 move to officially change its name to "Oppenheim's." By the early 1970s, the term *dry goods* was antiquated at best. At worst, few people under a certain age knew what it actually meant. As previously stated, the store's long, unwieldy name was often shortened by customers to the Dry, the Dry Goods or the Scranton Dry which was reflected in the store's revised 1960s logo. By the 1970s, store officials had decided the time had come to change the name to modernize the store's image and prepare for the company's impending expansion to areas outside of Scranton. The move was officially announced at a gala party at the local Sheraton Inn hosted by the Oppenheim family for longtime store associates and the local media for a night of dinner and dancing. The ballroom was bathed in the store's new colors of orange and yellow. These colors were considered chic compared to the dowdy green and gold that had been associated with the Dry for so long. To prevent confusion among its customers, the new logo included "Scranton Dry Goods Company" in small print below the Oppenheim name. Reaffirming her family's commitment, store president and family matriarch Constance Oppenheim said, "We dedicate ourselves and our organization to provide continued service to the people of our community."[220]

The lack of changes at The Globe and the multitude of changes at the Dry were two approaches that were simply prolonging the inevitable. The tides of change were barreling toward Scranton at breakneck speed, and no amount of renovation or remerchandising could stop them. Scranton's great department stores were about to face obstacles that, despite their best efforts, they could not overcome.

II

THE LADIES VANISH

As the sun set on the turbulent decade that was the 1960s and dawned on the 1970s, America had endured radical upheaval in the realms of politics, culture and morality. Seldom in the young nation's history had such titanic change taken place in a relatively short period of time. As everything once considered commonplace was changing rapidly, so was the fabric of the country's cities. Scranton, though spared much of the violent protests and rampant vandalism that other urban areas faced, was experiencing major shifts in its economy and population. The Globe Store and the Scranton Dry Goods Company, now called Oppenheim's, were beginning to suffer from these changes. Sales at the downtown stores began to seriously lag for the first time since the Great Depression. The Globe's parent company, John Wanamaker, did not invest in the store sufficiently to keep it updated and exciting. Oppenheim's downtown store, despite receiving a major renovation in the late 1960s, also began losing customers to nearby shopping plazas like Keyser-Oak. The company's much ballyhooed store in Mount Pocono, which would open in 1974, did not fare much better. The stores' circumstances seemed like they could not get much worse. In 1968, they did.

The new Viewmont Mall officially opened for business with great fanfare in February 1968. Located in neighboring Dickson City, the brand-new facility boasted 650,000 square feet of enclosed, climate-controlled shopping space and acres of free parking. Under its gigantic roof were twenty-one tenants, including a movie theater, restaurants, salons, shops and three major department stores: Sears, JCPenney and Grant City. Sears had eagerly abandoned its aged Adams Avenue store downtown to make the move to an ultramodern 155,000-square-foot space in the new mall that came with a separate auto center and large warehouse facilities. JCPenney returned to the region after a decade-long absence brought on by the closing of its Scranton store on North Washington Avenue in the late 1950s. Its two-story space and auto center at Viewmont encompassed 204,000 square feet and included a sit-down restaurant, hair salon, lawn-care center, toy shop and many other departments that could not be included in its former space downtown. Grant City, a subsidiary of W.T. Grant Company, was a discounter in the same league as S.S. Kresge's Kmart and Woolworth's. Crowds flocked to the mall to experience this new concept of shopping and were won over by the comforts, convenience and variety that it offered. Viewmont forever changed retailing in Northeastern Pennsylvania in a way that Scranton's venerable department store duo could not reverse.

On September 16, 1976, Grant's was officially replaced by Hess's of Allentown, Pennsylvania, when that store celebrated its grand opening at the Viewmont Mall. Under the brilliant and flamboyant leadership of its president, Max Hess Jr., Hess's had grown into a world-famous emporium. It was widely known for its daring marketing methods, international flower

The Viewmont Mall at Christmastime, circa 1970. *Courtesy of Greg Boock.*

shows, exotic fashions, frequent celebrity visits and Patio Restaurant located in its main store's basement. Its large downtown Allentown flagship consisted of six shopping levels that were resplendent with mirrors, marble, gold leaf and giant Bohemian crystal chandeliers. After it was sold in 1968 to Lehigh Valley businessman Philip I. Berman, Hess's began expanding to other areas of Pennsylvania, including Whitehall, Bethlehem, Easton, Lancaster, Wilkes-Barre, Harrisburg and Scranton. Berman continued many of Max Hess Jr.'s policies and practices before selling the company to mall developer Crown American in 1979. Crown American had built the Viewmont Mall and moved quickly to replace the outgoing Grant's with this flashy, forward-thinking retailer. Hess's was not shy about making its mark on Scranton and the other areas that it moved into. One of the most significant moves that the company made was its 1977 decision to intentionally violate Pennsylvania's Blue Laws, which dictated that nonessential businesses were to remain closed on Sundays, and open for business on the Christian Sabbath. Though the store was technically breaking the law with its Sunday opening, Hess's decision was made after Pennsylvania Supreme Court Justice Louis L. Manderino ordered that stores would not be prosecuted for the act. Moreover, the store's management felt that the potential profits from operating on Sunday far outweighed any potential controversy that Hess's opening would generate. Despite the public outcry from religious leaders, politicians and devout citizens, Hess's followed through on its plans. Hess's management was soon proven right. Its stores were jammed on Sundays, and the company made massive profits. The Globe and Oppenheim's, which had respected the Blue Laws since their founding, had to respond. Both stores began opening on Sunday, as did stores around the state. In a very short time, Hess's had proven to the local stalwarts that it was a force to be reckoned with.

Recognizing success, more shopping malls and plazas began popping up throughout Northeastern Pennsylvania. Like the Keyser Oak Shopping Center in Scranton, the Narrows Shopping Center opened in Edwardsville in the 1950s, siphoning businesses and customers away from downtown Wilkes-Barre. In 1971, Crown American, then known as Crown Construction, hoped to emulate its success in Scranton with an even more ambitious project in neighboring Wilkes-Barre Township. That year, the Wyoming Valley Mall opened with four anchor stores: Sears, JCPenney, Pomeroy's and Zollinger-Harned Company, an Allentown-based retailer. A few years later, Zollinger's was replaced by Hess's. In 1987, Pomeroy's parent company chose to focus its energy on the more modern suburban location and closed its downtown

Wilkes-Barre store. The mall's success led to a building boom around it that saw many retailers and shopping centers spring up around it. Like the Viewmont Mall, the Wyoming Valley's new retail center ushered in a new age of shopping in Northeastern Pennsylvania.

The Viewmont Mall's success had a similar effect in the Lackawanna Valley. In 1986, the rock face directly across from it was excavated to make way for the new Fashion Mall. A smaller outdoor shopping plaza, the Fashion Mall complemented Viewmont's offerings with a string of unique shops that offered anything from leather coats to fancy yogurts. Sugerman's, the former Eynon Drug Store, predated the new malls in 1961 by building an enormous superstore along Business Route 6, also known as the Scranton-Carbondale Highway, in nearby Eynon. With its reputation as a quirky one-stop shop that carried a large variety of goods—including fine furniture, clothing, hunting supplies, toys, electronics, appliances and lawn care—it was an instant hit in the Scranton area. So strong was its draw that locals coined the phrase "going up the Eynon" to describe their pilgrimage to this shopping mecca.

In addition to the Fashion Mall and Sugerman's, many other famous retail names made their home in the growing Dickson City shopping district. Discounter Zayre and S.S. Kresge's Kmart built large stores above the Viewmont Mall in 1973 to compete with Grant City. The following year, Kmart replaced another discounter, Arlans, on Birney Avenue in nearby Moosic, which had opened in 1970. These stores had the capability to sell large quantities of lower-end merchandise at excellent prices, which eventually ate away at the department stores' bargain basement business. Even Woolworth's had opened a large store in the nearby Keyser Oak Shopping Center in 1961 to complement its downtown operation. Across the lot, Keyser Oak's anchor Towers store went through a series of name changes, including Powers, Maxwell's, Pomeroy's and The Bon-Ton. With each change, the department store became slightly more upscale. Large toy stores came to the area with the opening of Kid's Toys at the Viewmont Mall, which was later succeeded by Kay-Bee Toys. In 1985, Children's Palace, a large toy retailer, opened a castle-like superstore on the overlook across from the mall. With their entire sales floors devoted to nothing but dolls, teddy bears, bicycles, video games and everything else a kid could want, these newcomers impressed area children in a way that the downtown stores' toy departments never could. Catalogue showrooms including Service Merchandise, Wes Freedman and Jewelcor also opened large, modern stores outside of the downtown during the 1970s and became strong competitors, particularly in the areas of jewelry and electronics. Adding to the competition provided by the big new stores in the area, The Globe, Oppenheim's and many of the other downtown retailers were forced to go head to head with smaller specialty stores that gradually chipped away at their clothing business. Trendy fashion-oriented shops like Lerner's (which itself had moved from Lackawanna Avenue to Viewmont), Fashion Bug and Suburban Casuals attracted young shoppers looking for hipper styles. Jean King, as its name suggests, concentrated on customers looking for something in denim. Established in 1977 by Wilkes-Barre businessman Elliot Katuna, Jean King joined the Viewmont lineup in 1981. It quickly became a popular addition to the many storefronts popping up in and around the mall. The tidal wave of retail that was building in Dickson City loomed ominously over downtown Scranton. As it crested and crashed, it washed away many of the city's oldest and most respected mercantile businesses.

The Globe and Oppenheim's continued to trudge forward throughout the 1970s amid the retailing onslaught brought on by the bustling businesses in Dickson City. Many of their smaller counterparts, however, were not as strong. From the 1970s to the 1990s, familiar names like Salben's, Schreiber's, Gloria Gelb Ltd, Ruth Ziman, Si Ferber, Scranton Talk and Joseph the Furrier moved or disappeared entirely. Household Outfitting Company was one of the most conspicuous vacant edifices when that company closed its nine-story Lackawanna Avenue store in 1963. Even Samters, the revered five-story clothier that had presided over the corner of Lackawanna and Penn Avenues for generations, closed its downtown store in May 1977 in favor of its more profitable locations at the Viewmont and Wyoming Valley Malls. The building briefly became a location for rival Jon York before closing for good one year later. With their newfound success as suburban big box stores, the reliable five-and-dimes S.S. Kresge's and Woolworth's shuttered their central city locations in 1982 and 1990, respectively. As the retail exodus gained momentum, Scranton's two largest stores found themselves increasingly alone in a dying downtown.

The Globe: Last Stop, Steamtown

In 1978, The Globe celebrated its one hundredth anniversary. The occasion was observed with yearlong celebrations and elaborate promotions. Giant banners, special packaging, birthday cakes, commemorative booklets, coins and wooden nickels all marked the festivities. A hot air balloon was chartered for a celebratory flight over Scranton, but poor weather prevented its takeoff. This did little to dampen the festivities as The Globe hosted a large parade and outdoor carnival on Wyoming Avenue that saw store employees dress in the styles that were popular when the store first opened. During that week, customers were also encouraged to dress up as if it were the nineteenth century and have their picture taken for a small fee. It was a very happy time for the store during an unhappy chapter in the city's history.

In 1979, William Russell Preston succeeded John A. Noble as president and CEO of The Globe Store. As the first leader to not be a descendant of the store's founders, Preston breathed new life into The Globe. Under Preston's leadership, a series of much needed changes, upgrades and renovations began at the aging institution. Becoming store president was the well-deserved pinnacle of Preston's career. He had earned his leadership position by being successful in various roles behind the counters, amid the aisles and in the executive offices of the retail business world.

Hailing from Youngstown, Ohio, W. Russell Preston built his retail career from the ground floor up. Preston was educated at Youngstown State University and the University of Cincinnati and served in the Army Air Corps during World War II.[221] After his education and wartime service, he secured a position as a salesman of men's furnishings at the G.M. McKelvey Company department store in downtown Youngstown. At McKelvey's, Preston rose through the ranks, becoming a buyer, a director of sales promotion and eventually the store's vice president and general merchandise manager. In 1967, McKelvey's named Preston as executive vice president and CEO. In 1972, Preston left McKelvey's to accept a position with the Globe Store as its executive vice president. Mimicking his success at McKelvey's, Preston rose through the executive ranks until he became The Globe's top official in 1979. The advent of Preston's tenure as the store's leader ushered in a new era of success for The Globe. Throughout the 1980s, Preston managed to buck the trend most downtown stores faced and greatly increased The Globe's annual sales volume, so much so that several sales records were broken.[222] He added several new and exciting sales events including "Surprise Saturday," "Secret Sale," and "Shop 'Til You Drop." New departments were also added, such as the "Mickey Mouse Shop" in 1986, which sold Disney-themed merchandise. One interesting department added under Preston's leadership was "Poppies"—a unique shop on the street floor spearheaded by Preston's wife, Peggy, that specialized in fresh flower arrangements. In addition to his duties at The Globe, Preston heavily invested himself in his new hometown by serving in many civic and business roles, including stints as general chairman of the Lackawanna United Way campaign, president of the Commercial Association of Scranton as well as the Credit Bureau of Scranton and treasurer and board member of Junior Achievement of Northeastern Pennsylvania.[223]

Globe Store President William Russell Preston. *Author's collection.*

On March 8, 1978, the John Wanamaker chain was sold by the Wanamaker family to Carter Hawley Hale Inc. for $60 million.[224] Carter Hawley Hale, a department store conglomerate based on the West Coast, had prevailed in a bidding war with Chicago's Marshall Field's to purchase the revered 117-year-old Philadelphia firm.[225] With prestigious names like San Francisco's Emporium, Los Angeles' The Broadway, Oakland's H.C. Capwell Co., Sacramento's Weinstock's, Dallas' Neiman Marcus and Manhattan's Bergdorf Goodman under its corporate umbrella, Carter Hawley Hale was a powerful and influential force in retail. According to noted retail historian Michael Lisicky, however, "Wanamaker's was Carter Hawley Hale's first traditional department store operation on the East Coast."[226] Despite its storied history, the new owners found that Wanamaker's had become a stodgy, old-fashioned institution with a reputation to match. Its conservative identity and failure to update its stores had allowed the competition to lure away customers. In addition, Wanamaker's had several outlets that were in undesirable locations.[227] To correct this, Lisicky states that Carter Hawley Hale invested $30 million over five years in updating Wanamaker's stores and merchandise offerings, most notably in its Philadelphia flagship store.[228] While Preston successfully steered The Globe to some of its greatest successes during the 1980s in terms of sales volume, Carter Hawley Hale still did not match the level of investment that was put into the store when it was under Cleland-Simpson's stewardship.

On November 4, 1986, as it was struggling to understand the East Coast customer and fending off hostile takeover attempts by Ohio-based women's clothier The Limited, Carter Hawley Hale gave up on Wanamaker's and sold

The Globe Store after the completion of the Wyoming Avenue Plaza project in 1978. *From the Mark Boock Collection. Courtesy of Greg Boock.*

the chain to Washington D.C.–based Woodward & Lothrop Department Stores for $183 million.[229] Woodward & Lothrop, or "Woodies" as it was called by many Washingtonians, had successfully beaten Allentown's Hess's and Wanamaker's own management for ownership of the firm.[230] Unlike Hess's, Woodies planned to keep the Wanamaker's name intact.[231] Perhaps more importantly, America's capital store offered far more money for Wanamaker's than Hess's did.[232] Moreover, Woodies had a history and big-city reputation to match Wanamaker's and seemed to be an ideal corporate partner for it. Unfortunately, Woodies, like Wanamaker's, had become outdated and outclassed in the glitzy yet vicious world of 1980s retail and was beginning to falter. As its owner, Detroit shopping mall magnate A. Alfred Taubman, had incurred massive debt with large purchases—including the Wanamaker's chain—Woodies could not invest the funds needed to fully restore The Globe to its former glory. Preston and his management team realized this and decided that a major move was needed to run the store their way. The great risk of their make-or-break move would either ensure The Globe's future or spell its doom.

As Wanamaker's and Woodward & Lothrop were failing, W. Russell Preston and The Globe's management team began aspiring to purchase The Globe and save it from its parent company's downward spiral. In 1987, the Globe Acquisition Group was formed consisting of Preston,

Happy New Year!

We want to take this opportunity to wish all of you, our customers and friends in Scranton and Northeastern Pennsylvania, a very happy and prosperous New Year in 1988. At the same time, we want to thank you for helping make 1987 such a memorable year. Some of the highlights of 1987 were:

The purchase of The Globe in May by local investors bringing ownership back to Scranton.

The achievement of our biggest sales day ever on December 5, 1987, when we exceeded $1,000,000 in sales.

Sales for the month of December set another all time record.

Our company received national recognition as one of the best retail stores in the country.

The remodeling of our Charl-Mont Restaurant was just the first step in our plans to completely remodel our store interior during the next several years. Soon you will begin to see a completely new look take place on our 4th and 5th floors as the next step in this ongoing process.

None of this would have been possible without your enthusiastic and loyal support.

In 1988, we pledge to you that we will continue to bring you the best and most complete merchandise assortments anywhere, combined with the very finest customer service it is possible to give.

Again, our heartfelt thanks to all of you for helping us achieve these important milestones and we look forward to serving you even better in 1988 and the years ahead.

Sincerely,

W. Russell Preston
Chairman of the Board and C.E.O.

A letter by W. Russell Preston to customers after the store was acquired by the Globe Acquisition Group in 1987. *Author's collection.*

The Globe's senior vice president William A. Buck, former Pennsylvania governor William Warren "Bill" Scranton and several other local businesspeople including six top executives from Haddon Craftsmen Inc., a Scranton book bindery. On May 5, 1987, the group's leveraged buyout of The Globe was completed for $12 million. After nearly nineteen years operating as a division of an out-of-town company, The Globe was once again under local control.

With the acquisition deal inked, the Globe Acquisition Group had bold plans to renovate and modernize the aged store. Over the next several years, $2 million was spent to renovate, revamp and redecorate all divisions of The Globe. The first and fourth floors received the most attention, the latter of which became The Globe's new "Youth Center." New carpeting, lighting and display fixtures were installed to create "Northeastern Pennsylvania's most complete Youth Center for fashion clothing and accessories for infants, toddlers, children, teens, juniors, and young men!"[233] As a result of the work, the furniture department was eliminated while floor coverings, window treatments, the sleep shop, electronics, televisions and stereos were moved to the fifth floor. On the first floor, the men's department was moved to a new space in the main store while its former location, the Hotel Jermyn annex, was closed. The Charl-Mont Restaurant, still a favorite dining spot among locals, also received a complete makeover. The store's new upscale look, updated merchandise offerings and strong sales volume earned it widespread recognition and strengthened its sterling reputation for class and service. In December 1987, a high-profile court battle involving a popular perfume brand unintentionally gave The Globe a huge amount of free publicity when the presiding judge named the store as one of the classiest in the United States. His rendered opinion ranked The Globe Store alongside the likes of Saks Fifth Avenue, Bergdorf Goodman, Bullocks Wilshire and Barney's New York.[234] As the 1980s drew to a close, The Globe's future looked bright to the outside observer, but internal forces were slowly but surely pulling the store apart at the seams.

Despite the store's continued success under W. Russell Preston's leadership, it soon became clear that The Globe was in serious financial trouble after the buyout. To purchase the store, the Globe Acquisition Group had accumulated enormous debt that was weighing heavily on the store's bottom line. Wading in red ink, the group sold The Globe in 1991 to Edward G. Rossi, one of the members of the 1987 acquisition group. Rossi was a Clarks Summit businessman who had built his career at Haddon Craftsman, eventually rising to the rank of executive vice president. Shortly after the

Left: A 1988 Globe advertisement highlighting the store's new "Youth Center" on the fourth floor. *Author's collection.*

Right: A 1988 advertisement showcasing the newly renovated Charl-Mont Restaurant. *Author's collection.*

store was sold to Rossi, Preston stepped down as board chairman and cut all ties to The Globe Store citing "management differences."[235] Preston had recently been named "Retailer of the Year" by the Pennsylvania Retailers Association. The honor was well-deserved, as The Globe was designated as one of the top one hundred department stores in the country in 1990 by *Stores* magazine. Except for Bergdorf Goodman, The Globe was the only single-unit department store in the country to make the list with a respectable $26 million in sales. The loss of W. Russell Preston's leadership left The Globe adrift like a ship without a rudder.

As part of The Globe deal, the city agreed to provide a $1 million loan under the U.S. Department of Housing and Urban Development's Section 108 of the Community Development Block Grant Program as well as an additional $300,000 loan from the state. Sadly, the city pulled funding earmarked for the restoration of the Hotel Casey to provide the loan to The

Globe. Its rebirth snatched from it in the eleventh hour, the Hotel Casey's once grand and soaring interiors became more hideously transformed each year thanks to vandals, neglect and the elements. Eventually, the one-time monarch of Lackawanna Avenue became too far gone to save and the Casey was mercifully demolished in 2001. As for The Globe, Rossi had big plans for the store, including major renovations and remerchandising of all departments. In 1991, he stated to the local media, "I'm upgrading everything, from pots and pans to women's dresses and men's suits. We have to bring it back to be more like Lord & Taylor or Bloomingdale's, where people want to come downtown."[236]

To show that progress was being made, one of Rossi's first moves was to change the store's name to "The New Globe." In a self-congratulatory nod to its status as Scranton's oldest and largest department store, the new logo was bold enough to ask, "Where else?" in print advertising. Unfortunately for Rossi and The New Globe, Northeastern Pennsylvania shoppers had many answers to that question. The burgeoning business districts on the Scranton-Carbondale Highway in Dickson City and Kidder Street in Wilkes-Barre Township provided many more modern and convenient alternatives to the aged downtown stores. Outnumbered and outrivaled, The Globe was fighting a losing battle.

The Globe's one saving grace was the eagerly anticipated Mall at Steamtown. Spearheaded by Reading, Pennsylvania department store magnate Albert "Al" Boscov, the new mall promised to bring new shops to Scranton in an ultramodern facility that would boast two shopping levels, above and below ground parking and two new anchor stores—Boscov's and Montgomery Ward. The Globe would be connected to the new mall via a large pedestrian bridge, which the store dubbed the "Fashion Bridge," that would seamlessly connect to the historic building on the second floor. Designed so customers traversing the bridge would not sense that they were hovering over the busy traffic on Lackawanna Avenue, the new walkway would have an interior that was modeled to serve as additional selling space for the store. Hence its name, the proposed downtown shopping center would tie-in both in theme and function to the adjacent Steamtown National Historic Site, which had been in development since the mid-1980s. Utilizing the old Scranton Railyards, roundhouse, and service buildings, the site was being redeveloped into an interactive museum focusing on the area's extensive railroad history. The centerpiece of the museum was the large collection of vintage trains, then known as "Steamtown USA," which had been acquired from a Vermont collector in the mid-1980s. To accompany

Historic buildings along Lackawanna Avenue are imploded in 1992 to make way for the construction of the Mall at Steamtown. *From the Mark Boock Collection. Courtesy of Greg Boock.*

the collection, countless artifacts relating to the railroad industry were gathered to put on display in the new museum.

Time and again throughout the 1980s, many complications delayed the building of the Mall at Steamtown. Al Boscov, however, was an extremely determined and tireless businessman with an unsinkable optimism that saw the project through. Finally, after years of red tape and legal battles with local property owners, the mall project took a huge step forward when on April 5, 1992, the historic buildings that lined Lackawanna Avenue were imploded in a spectacular display that was heavily promoted and broadcast live on local news outlets as well as nationally on CNN. To celebrate the event, The Globe held an "Implosion Sale"; for one day only, all merchandise was marked down 20 percent. Construction on the mall began shortly thereafter.

On October 23, 1993, the $101 million Mall at Steamtown officially opened to the public with pomp and show. On hand for the grand opening ceremonies were *The Dick Van Dyke Show* alum Morey Amsterdam and singing star Patty Andrews of the famed Andrews Sisters. The event drew as many as seventy thousand people, and with the cutting of a red ribbon by Pennsylvania Governor Bob Casey Sr. and other dignitaries, the crowds excitedly piled into the mall's bright and airy concourse. Rays of sunshine flooded its interior thanks to the designers' copious use of skylights. To add to the celebratory mood, special events, sales and exhibits including a $250,000 collection of classic film costumes from the golden age of MGM Studios were scheduled throughout the grand opening weekend. After waiting for nearly a decade for the mall project to come to fruition, downtown merchants finally had reason to believe that the city's renaissance had begun.

Despite the excitement surrounding the opening of the Mall at Steamtown and the increase in customer traffic downtown, The Globe was struggling to keep its head above water. Interestingly, the store had one final logo change during this time. The longtime script was dropped, as was the "new" moniker, in favor of a simple, elegant block letter logo that fit the simplistic modernity of the 1990s. Notwithstanding its trendiness, the new logo seemed out of place when associated with a store steeped in so much history. Contrary to intentions, the new logo represented a lack of life and energy at the old institution. Despite all the efforts of the city, mall developers, management, staff and the revolving door of store leaders who tried to reverse its decline, The Globe was dying.

The Globe's story came to a sudden end on January 27, 1994. On that cold, crisp morning, customers began filling the store's heated entrance lobby waiting for the main doors to be unlocked at the normal opening time. To their shock and dismay, they found a simple black and white sign taped to the glass that coldly signaled the end of era: "STORE CLOSED." Globe employees, most of whom had reported to work with no knowledge of the impending closure, were told they were out of a job at a 10:00 a.m. meeting of all store associates. Blindsided by the announcement, they hastily gathered their belongings into shopping bags and retrieved their final paychecks. Approximately 286 full- and part-time associates, many of whom had been with the store for decades, were either forced into retirement or to search for work elsewhere. The Charl-Mont Restaurant, which had become locally owned following Price Candy Company's 1982 sale, served its last customers and was forced to lock its doors as well. Several who had shopped The Globe for their entire lives expressed a genuine sense of sadness and loss. One longtime customer commented, "I'm going to miss it very much; it's been here so long."[237] Another said, "It's a damn shame....It's been a landmark in town as long as I can remember."[238] The closing came after the store and its assets were seized by

PNC Bank, the company's major credit holder. The crushing debt, which had not been cleared since the acquisition group purchased the store from John Wanamaker in 1987, coupled with high rent, excessive overhead, the Blizzard of 1993 and an inability to acquire additional capital, adversely affected profits to the point where The Globe was no longer a solvent business. At the time of the closing, store owner Edward Rossi stated that the store was in debt for $11 million.[239] Of the $11 million debt, $5 million was owed to the bank, another $5 million was owed to Scranton Mall Associates, the owners of the Mall at Steamtown, and $1 million was owed to the Scranton Office of Economic Development.[240] In addition to the major debt, The Globe owed money to over 1,000 other creditors.[241] One Scranton newspaper reported the number as much higher, at about 3,900 creditors.[242] During the subsequent bankruptcy proceedings, it was stated by several witnesses that the store would not have been able to pay its employees had it remained open for one more day.[243]

Throughout the following months, a $6 million liquidation sale was held to rid the building of its remaining merchandise. The stock's sale was approved by a federal bankruptcy court judge who granted control of The Globe's final sale days to Ohio-based Jubilee Limited Partnership. In April 1994, with most of its merchandise gone, the last sale of The Globe's existence was held to sell off the store's furniture and fixtures. Those in charge of the fixture sale exclaimed that "everything and anything in the 260,000 square foot store that isn't nailed down can and will be sold."[244] In a ghostly echo of its glory days, people jammed the first floor in a feeding frenzy to grab a good deal on anything left in the nearly empty emporium. Moving trucks, station wagons and any other suitable vehicles lined up in front of the building in a macabre choreography to receive anything from a few trinkets and souvenirs to piles of furniture, mannequins, cash registers, clothing racks and display cases. In addition, many aged and historic items were found in the store after the closing. Unusual for a large business, Globe management and staff had a habit of storing antique fixtures and merchandise in the store's labyrinth of stockrooms, closets and storage spaces. Among the items found were 1910s-era Victorian dolls used in long-ago window displays and a 1920s-era hat rack. Vintage furniture, camera equipment, train sets and sewing machines were also found by the liquidation staff. The president of the liquidation firm said at the time that "there's 138 years of stuff loaded in this building….It's a real interesting old place, they've locked away the past."[245] During the sale, store manager Joe Hulbirt took the opportunity to say goodbye to former customers. When asked to describe what The Globe's last months in business were like, he said that it reminded him of waiting for a "terminal patient to die."[246]

Filled with memories of a glorious past and a thriving city, The Globe's only patrons were now those heading for the basement to pay their final installments on their store charge accounts or those raiding the store for anything of value. Many others just wanted to take a final look before the doors closed forever. Recognizing the historical significance of the moment, Boscov's ran a full-page advertisement in the local newspaper that summed up the feelings of many local residents:

> *Like everyone else in Lackawanna County, we were shocked and saddened by the news that our good friend and neighbor, The Globe Store, had made the difficult decision to close its doors. After 116 years of outstanding service to the community, it's hard to say goodbye. We respected The Globe as an honorable competitor, we admired their staff of talented and dedicated co-workers and we loved to eat in their wonderful restaurant. Certainly, The Globe will be missed by all of us.*[247]

The Dry: November 1, 1980

The Dry's ending was just as painful to the area. Since the mid-1970s, the company's profits were in serious decline. Despite high hopes, the Mount Pocono store failed. It was unceremoniously closed in 1979 after only forty-nine months of operation. At the time, Secretary-Treasurer Richard Oppenheim said, "Our Mount Pocono store just never came up to the sales figures that the marketing research people anticipated."[248] After over a decade of relative success despite its small size, the Clarks Summit Country Store was also closed in 1979, and the property was sold for $115,000. These measures were taken in large part to generate working capital for the company and to enable management to focus on the flagship store, which itself was ailing in a deteriorating downtown.

To improve the crumbling image of downtown Scranton, a bold proposal was put forth in 1974 to turn the 100 block of Wyoming Avenue into a pedestrian mall. Several business owners in the area championed the idea, and the major retailers, including Oppenheim's executive vice-president Ellis Oppenheim and Globe Store executive vice-president W. Russell Preston, spearheaded its development. In addition, Oppenheim served as official spokesman for the mall project and often took the role of intermediary between the local media, business owners and city leaders. Controversy and bitter in-fighting between businesses and city leaders over the type of mall that should be built, however, significantly delayed construction. In a memorandum to Scranton's political and business leaders titled "There Is a Crisis in Our City," Oppenheim summed up the problems facing the city's business district and implored its leaders to act:

> *Our young people are leaving because of a lack of opportunities. "For Rent" signs are becoming more prevalent. We are losing what was once a thriving center of commercial, professional, financial, and recreational activity. Without a viable center city, you cannot have a viable city or a viable county. You cannot attract the right industrial prospects, only those on the fringe. We must act and act now! We must do so in an innovative and forceful manner, cooperatively, without pettiness or partisanship. All segments must pull together.*[249]

In May 1978, construction on the downtown mall finally began at a cost of $862,000 and was completed later the same year. The "Wyoming Avenue Plaza," as the mall was christened, transformed the 100 block of Wyoming Avenue into a tree-lined, pedestrian-friendly thoroughfare complete with decorative planters, comfortable seating, improved lighting, advertising kiosks, artistic sculptures, granite safety bollards, a clock tower and a playground for children. The street itself was given a sophisticated look thanks to the use of interlocking rustic-colored brick pavers. Solid granite curbs and rustic-colored pavers with concrete bands tied the look of the sidewalks to the street. Despite all the new additions and changes, the existing four lanes of the 100 block of Wyoming Avenue were maintained, and Scranton's COLTS bus service continued to pick up and drop off passengers regularly at the front entrances of The Globe and Oppenheim's via newly constructed bus pull offs.

To improve the store's chances of long-term survival, nationally recognized department store merchandising expert Michael Hayes joined the company in 1978 as its general merchandise manager. Hayes had extensive experience and had successfully served in similar roles at C.K. Whitner & Co. in Reading, Pennsylvania; Harvey's of Nashville, Tennessee; Higbee's of Cleveland, Ohio; and O'Neil's in Akron, Ohio. In 1979, he was promoted to vice president in charge of merchandising at Oppenheim's, the first to hold such a role who was not related to the Dry's founder, Ike Oppenheim.

An Oppenheim's advertisement showcasing the features of the new Wyoming Avenue Plaza in 1978. *Author's collection.*

Although Hayes replaced Ellis Sr. in that position, Ike's eldest son continued as a leader of the company in the role of executive vice president for the remainder of its run.

Despite these efforts, Oppenheim's continued to struggle. As the 1970s drew to a close, the situation became so dire that the Oppenheim family had to repeatedly inject monies from personal funds into the store just to keep it running. In the first ten months of fiscal year 1978 alone, the company lost $820,425.[250] The Dry's business state had become unsustainable, and in 1979, the company was forced to file for Chapter XI bankruptcy protection. Approved by bankruptcy judge Thomas C. Gibbons, the plan allowed for Scranton Dry Goods Co. Inc., the parent company of the Oppenheim's store, to continue its retail operations without interruption. The plan also froze all the company's debt, which prevented immediate legal action by its creditors. To pay its creditors, Oppenheim's obtained a mortgage on the downtown store, which would allow it to pay $0.30 on the dollar to its unsecured creditors over six payments.[251] To pay two secured loans that amounted to over $1.5 million, the store would refinance its accounts receivable and use its fixtures, furniture and equipment as collateral.[252] A new financing plan was put into place soon after to enable the company to replenish its dwindling stock in time for the 1979 holiday shopping season. Ellis Oppenheim enthusiastically stated to the local media that "we've been downtown for 67 years, and we're not going to leave now."[253] His brother, Richard, added that the disappointing performance of the Mount Pocono store "coupled with delays in finishing the Downtown Mall [*sic*], produced a cash flow problem. This, in turn, left us short of merchandise during the crucial holiday gift-buying season. Now, with our new financing plans and a little breathing space, we'll be stocking up all six floors of our Scranton store in order to have a successful 1979."[254]

Despite the initial optimism, the bankruptcy filing confirmed rumors that the Dry was in desperate financial straits. This became painfully obvious to customers, who noticed departments quietly close down or be drastically reduced in size and scope, including toys, furniture and major appliances. The staff, once numbering over eight hundred during peak shopping periods, had dwindled to around fifty. In addition, the company began to have difficulty affording consistent advertising, which further hurt its ability to attract customers. In 1980, talk among locals familiar with Oppenheim's changed from the store's unhealthy financial situation to its seemingly inevitable closure.

Oppenheim's one chance at survival hinged on the redevelopment of the historic store building into a vertical mall. Dubbed as the "Galleria," the new mall would feature various shops and restaurants situated around a circular indoor courtyard that would lead from the street floor to the roof. Kresge's, Woolworth's and several other neighboring buildings along Wyoming Avenue would be purchased and incorporated into the $10 million project. In addition, Oppenheim's 250-space parking garage would be expanded to accommodate 600 cars. Oppenheim's itself would retrench and become a "junior" department store while continuing to serve as a downtown anchor. Championed by Mayor Eugene Hickey, the Galleria

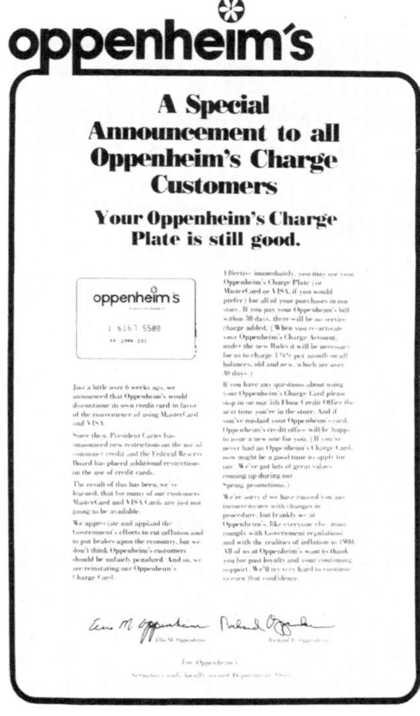

Shortly before its 1980 closing, Oppenheim's decided to discontinue its in-house credit card. Company officials quickly reversed their decision when they found many customers would not have access to cards from national credit companies after new government regulations were put in place to halt inflation. *Author's collection.*

Mall was hoped to revitalize not only Oppenheim's, but the entire downtown business district.

Those hopes were dashed on November 1, 1980. That Saturday had begun like any other business day. The employees reported to work at their normal start times. The lights were turned on. The counters were uncovered. The cash registers were prepared for the day's transactions. The big glass doors were unlocked. A steady stream of customers filed in. Despite the bleak rumors swirling around the store, there was no indication that this day would be different from any other. That changed abruptly at around 4:00 p.m., when the remaining employees were called to a meeting on the street floor in front of the escalators. There, store leader Ellis Oppenheim stood on the now stationary stairway overlooking the crowd and made the announcement that the sixty-eight-year-old family business would be closing forever in thirty minutes. An instant wave of shock and sadness washed over the crowd, many of whom had called the Dry home for all their working lives. The store's last customers, looking just as shocked and befuddled as the staff, made their last purchases and left. The doors were bolted shut behind them, leaving last-minute shoppers standing in the entrance lobby to observe the funereal atmosphere within. As employees gathered their belongings into shopping bags and emotionally said their last goodbyes, news reporters were waiting for them at the exits. Rumors that the store was closing had reached the local newsrooms, which immediately sent journalists to cover the historic event. Among those interviewed on their way out was Olga Gowka, who for just shy of fifty years had served as a buyer in the women's department. With tears streaming down her face, she said, "They [the Oppenheim family] were wonderful people….I feel rotten, just rotten."[255] Another was Moe Popkin, a twenty-year veteran of the store, who said, "It was a great organization, great people to work for…something like this takes a lot out of you."[256] Customers echoed the same sentiments with statements like "I can't believe it" and "Boy, this is the end of an era…it's a shame." [257] As the last employees left and disappeared into the autumn night, the store went completely dark save for a few lights left on that gave the street floor a dim, ghostly look. The Dry was gone. I.E. Oppenheim's dream was over.

Oppenheim's sudden closure greatly discouraged the developers of the Galleria Mall project. They were no longer as interested in taking a risk on a downtown mall now that their sure anchor was no more and eventually canceled their plans by 1983. To rid the store of its furniture and fixtures, the Dry's last official sale took the form of an auction a few months later in April 1981. Like vultures picking over the carcass of a dead giant, eager bargain hunters crowded the store one last time to bid on clothing racks, shelving units, holiday displays, mail machines, cash registers, brooms, ironing boards, trash bags and, of course, Santa's throne. The remaining merchandise had been sold to a retail firm based in Binghamton, New York, for $133,000. Now completely empty, the old neoclassical edifice faced the 1980s with an uncertain future. As for the business itself, locals lamented the loss of one of their favorite area stores and a reliable stalwart of the downtown. In his weekly commentary for the *Scranton Times*, Joseph X. Flannery gave a warm reflection on the Dry:

> *My earliest recollections of the store is that it was always crowded. The bells of the cash registers, the popping sound of the pneumatic tube system, the conversations of customers and clerks, the click-click noises of the escalators, the periodic paging of store officials, the metallic noise of the elevator doors closing and—ever so often—the wail of a lost child made an impression on my mind that I can still recall…and now the Scranton Dry is just another memory. But it's a pleasant memory, nonetheless.*[258]

12

GRAND REOPENING

After The Globe and the Dry closed, their huge buildings sat vacant for years. Like two fading dowagers desperately clinging to their last shreds of dignity, their grime- and soot-coated façades stood as sad monuments to Scranton's dismal economy. City officials tried to bring excitement and activity to the former department stores with varying degrees of success. Nevertheless, their vast, empty sales floors grew decrepit as they echoed with the memories of a more prosperous era.

The Globe: Reimagining and Diversifying

Once home to the best merchandise that could be found in Northeastern Pennsylvania, The Globe stood largely vacant and forlorn during the latter part of the 1990s. During the annual Saint Patrick's Day Parade, however, the store came alive again, albeit in a much different role. For a time, The Globe served as a stable for the Budweiser Clydesdale horses that made an appearance in the parade. Where gleaming counters once stood containing the latest in fine fragrances, cosmetics and jewelry, the reddish-brown and white equines grazed on straw that was strewn about the terrazzo floors. Prior to the parade, local horse enthusiasts were allowed back into the store to get a close-up view of these massive and majestic animals. Thanks to the Clydesdales, The Globe briefly reclaimed its status as a major draw to downtown.

The Globe Store sits vacant and forlorn in the late 1990s. Note the pine trees that were still in place above the main entrance from the store's final Christmas season in 1994. *Author's collection.*

In 1994, another department store bucked the trend of large retailers avoiding downtowns and briefly considered The Globe as its next location. Seeking to expand to the Scranton area, Kaufmann's of Pittsburgh, Pennsylvania, was looking for a space large enough to accommodate its needs and be part of a major shopping complex. As it was comparable to The Globe in terms of quality and scope, Kaufmann's seemed to be the perfect fit as the third anchor in the Mall at Steamtown. Unfortunately for the city, Kaufmann's parent company, May Department Stores Company of St. Louis, purchased several stores from the defunct Hess's chain in 1995 and instead chose to take its place at the Viewmont Mall. Strawbridge & Clothier, John Wanamaker's former archrival in Philadelphia, was also envisioned by city officials as a worthy successor to The Globe. That store's 1996 sale to the May Department Stores Company, however, erased any hope of it becoming a downtown tenant. Even Walmart briefly considered The Globe as a temporary location in 1996 after its Dickson City store was heavily damaged by falling boulders from Bell Mountain. Ultimately, however, officials from that company chose a different building that was more compatible with their business model.

To better control what the huge store would become, the city purchased The Globe building from the Simpson estate in 1994 for $2.4 million. A major stumbling block to the building's redevelopment at that point was the fact that The Globe had so many owners. Prior to the city deal, the Simpson family still held the deed to the store structure and the attached Easy Park garage. By the 1990s, the number of heirs to the Simpson estate had swelled to fifty people. The city's purchase of The Globe from these heirs would make any redevelopment deal far less complicated. While the city searched for a new tenant, preferably another large department store, the Easy Park garage was renamed the Electric City garage and reopened to the public. A few years later, it was physically connected to a new movie theater and parking deck next door, effectively doubling its capacity. Around this time, the Lackawanna County Chamber of Commerce produced an advertising video that touted The Globe as a prime business location to potential suitors. Despite this effort, The Globe building remained stubbornly vacant.

It was not until 1997 that The Globe's fortunes changed. That year, Diversified Records Inc., a records management company, expressed real interest in relocating their main offices and operations to the former department store. Thinking "outside the box," Scranton Mayor James "Jim" Connors lobbied Diversified's founder and president Clifford Melberger to consider The Globe as his company's new corporate headquarters.[259] Impressed by the size, location and grandeur of the building, Melberger and his wife were sold on the store.[260] On July 29, 1997, Diversified made the formal announcement that they would purchase The Globe and renovate it into a state-of-the-art corporate office and storage facility. According to Melberger, he specifically requested that his office be in the same location on the fifth floor where he had visited Santa Claus as a child.[261] On September 28, 1998, a ribbon-cutting ceremony attended by Melberger, Connors, Pennsylvania Governor Tom Ridge and other city and state officials officially reopened The Globe as Diversified's Metrotech Center. Renovations to the building included records storage space in the basement and part of the street floor. In addition, the street floor held space for retail and office purposes as well as a small area for the Everhart Museum to display artwork. Floors two through four would also serve as available office space while Diversified's own offices occupied the fifth and sixth floors.

The Diversified deal was a boon for Scranton. The company brought eight hundred full- and part-time jobs to the city with annual salaries ranging from $20,000 to $30,000 on average, a respectable rate in 1998. The new company, later known as Diversified Information Technologies, thrived in the store until 2014. That year, its new parent company, EDM Americas, chose to relocate the corporate headquarters to its facilities on nearby Montage Mountain.

After Diversified moved out in 2014, The Globe was once again a vacant building. It remained a darkened monolith until 2015, when a holiday display consisting of store memorabilia collected from area residents reignited interest in the property. Local business owner and Scranton Tomorrow board member Joshua Mast was inspired to organize the project after hearing several local residents describe their memories of the store to him. Enjoying the nostalgia of holidays past, the public eagerly embraced the display. The popularity of the event attracted the attention of Lackawanna County officials who were in the market for a centralized location for most county offices and business. The Globe, with its over 250,000 square feet of space and attached parking garage, was perfect for the role. A year later, Lackawanna County Commissioners voted to purchase the building for $1.3 million and turn it into a central hub for county government offices. Previously, the county had offices scattered around the city in numerous buildings which made leasing space complicated and accessibility for residents confusing and difficult. At a cost of approximately $17 million, the building was renovated so that the street floor could accommodate courtrooms, voter registration offices and the Veterans Affairs department. The second floor was revamped so offices for tax claims, single-tax, recorder of deeds, accessor, treasurer and controller could take up residence on the former center of women's fashions for the store. The upper floors were made to include space for other county government agencies and functions, including the Lackawanna Human Development Agency, Office of Youth and Family Services, Area Agency on Aging, County Solicitor, Domestic Relations, Community Relations and the Health and Human Services Office. To celebrate the structure's past, the county undertook several efforts to honor the store's memory. As a permanent homage to the former department store, Lackawanna County collected store memorabilia from the public, including fine coats, boxes, bags and Rudi Bears for a display on the street floor. Additionally, a space was set aside for a small eatery that would bear the "Charl-Mont" name. Unfortunately, the resurrected Charl-Mont restaurant did not last and closed a short time after its grand opening. In a final nod of respect, the building was renamed the Lackawanna County Government Center at The Globe. For the first time since 1994, The Globe's distinctive script logo would once again grace the Wyoming Avenue entranceway.

The Dry: A Phoenix from the Ashes

The Dry's fortunes have also dramatically improved in the years since the store closed in November 1980. During the early 1980s, however, its future looked quite grim. As it spent the Reagan era empty, its condition steadily declined. The years of vandalism, neglect and harsh Northeastern Pennsylvania winters took a serious toll on the structure. Its majesty was grotesquely transformed as the roof leaked, pipes froze and broke, windows were shattered, doors were boarded up and vegetation grew from its entrance marquees. Despite its sad state, its neoclassical façade maintained an odd, lingering beauty as its intricate details continued to show through the deterioration.

Like it did with The Globe a decade later, Scranton attempted to fill the Dry's empty halls with anything that would bring excitement and attention to the corner of Lackawanna and Wyoming Avenues, however ephemeral. With its purchase of the building for $200,000, the city reluctantly inherited the exorbitant costs of maintaining and heating the aged goliath. It quickly grew anxious to fill the Dry with another tenant. In November 1981, the people of Scranton elected James Barrett "Jim" McNulty as its next mayor. McNulty was a colorful character as a politician with a jovial, fun-loving attitude and a flair for promotion. His practice of giving away roses to those he met became his trademark and helped endear him to the city's residents. As its darkened presence loomed menacingly over one of the most visible areas of the downtown, restoring the Dry to its former glory was an immediate priority for the McNulty administration. This was demonstrated very early on as the new mayor chose the store and the street corner in front of it as the setting for his inaugural festivities. After being inaugurated at city hall on January 4, 1982, the new mayor triumphantly made his way to Wyoming Avenue, where cheering crowds were waiting to greet him. Speeches, fireworks and a general feeling of renewal were the order of the evening. With the cutting of a ribbon, the Dry's doors were thrown open and the mayor's guests marched in; a sea of tables, linens, chairs and balloons took the place of counters, perfumes and clothes racks. Visitors dined and danced throughout the night, which briefly reinvigorated the otherwise lifeless store. The optics of this celebration were not lost on the McNulty administration. The new mayor hoped that filling the store with people would help attract the interest of another department store company.

Unlike outgoing Mayor Eugene Hickey, McNulty eschewed the idea of a galleria of shops in favor of a full-line department store that could match

The Globe in scale and scope. At the top of his list were local store chains Pomeroy's and Boscov's. Pomeroy's, itself contending with aging downtown locations in Wilkes-Barre and Reading, never expressed any real interest in the Oppenheim's Building or downtown Scranton. Al Boscov, however, did not immediately slam the door on McNulty's proposal to locate a store in the city. Boscov had found unexpected success in downtown Wilkes-Barre when he assumed ownership of the moribund Fowler, Dick and Walker—The Boston Store. So successful was his version of the revamped Boston Store, Boscov later spearheaded a project to turn Wilkes-Barre's dilapidated Paramount Theater into the F.M Kirby Center for the Performing Arts as a thank-you to the people of that city. Boscov knew that he could replicate that success in downtown Scranton, but not with the Dry. Instead, he planned to build a new mall by Memorial Stadium near the North Scranton Expressway and outside of the city's central business district.

Undeterred, McNulty undertook several attempts to fill the Dry and attract attention to its availability. The most notable of these attempts was when he temporarily turned the Dry into a training ground for boxing great Larry Holmes in 1983. Preparing for his upcoming "Homecoming" match against rival Lucien Rodriguez at the Watres Armory, Holmes utilized the huge second floor to set up a full training ring. Additional space was made available for the 700 to 1,500 daily onlookers who, for a nominal donation to Steamtown USA, could have a front-row seat to watch the heavyweight champion train. They could also purchase tickets for the big fight that was to take place in March of that year. When asked about the odd setup in the vacant department store, Mayor McNulty responded, "We moved the lingerie out and moved Larry in."[262]

Another noteworthy effort to fill the Dry with activity was the addition of the "Miniature Memories" train display, which, by the early 1980s, had already become a favorite attraction, having been in other spaces throughout the area. In the Dry, the display's creator, Don Clark, utilized the first floor and mezzanine to set up his miniaturized version of Scranton, which included local landmarks such as the Tunkhannock Viaduct, Scranton City Hall, Everhart Museum and the Lackawanna Train Station. Many yards of HO-, O- and N-scale track snaked their way around the scaled-down city on which Clark's extensive collection of vintage model trains chugged and whistled. In addition, the street floor featured a small movie house, a souvenir shop and a large train ride for children. The attraction proved popular, particularly around the holidays. Other events staged at the Dry included Halloween parties, window painting contests, blood drives, health fairs, flea markets, a car show, a disaster relief sign-up for those affected by Hurricane Gloria in 1985 and a large sale of fine crystal and silver from the neighboring Helen Schwartz Gifts when that store sustained heavy damage during a 1982 fire.

Building on these efforts, Jim McNulty persistently lobbied Al Boscov to move into Oppenheim's. He even offered the city's help in expanding and renovating the building and its parking garage to accommodate Boscov's needs. Boscov was unmoved. He did not think the age, setup and size of the Dry were conducive to the needs of a modern department store. Moreover, the store's less than ideal parking setup served to further discourage him. Boscov's vision for Scranton was for a new mall that could realistically take on Viewmont and the surrounding businesses in Dickson City. His desire to build outside of the downtown, however, did not align with the vision of Scranton city leaders, who felt that that development would devastate what remained of the central business district. As early as 1981, Mayor Eugene Hickey stressed to Boscov that his idea to build a mall adjacent to Memorial Stadium ran counter to the city's revitalization plan and urged him to reconsider a site in the central city. The two sides compromised during the administration of McNulty's successor, Mayor David J. Wenzel, by creating a plan for a downtown mall along Lackawanna Avenue that would tie in to the adjacent Steamtown National Historic Site, which was also under development at the time. Dubbed the "Lackawanna Avenue Mall Project," the developers' agreement to build the mall was formally signed on August 24, 1988, during a ceremony held on the street floor of the Dry. Ever the optimist, Boscov believed that the new mall's success would spill over and improve other areas of the city. Thus, Boscov included the Dry and the vacant Samters buildings in his plans for redevelopment. In December 1989, Scranton Mall Associates, the corporation established by Boscov and others to handle the mall's construction, also purchased the Lewis & Reilly building for $225,000 so it could be included in the revitalization effort. Unlike their previous incarnations as retail outlets, Boscov planned to turn the Dry, Lewis & Reilly, and Samters into state-of-the-art office complexes that would draw high-paying professional jobs to the city. Despite his persistence, the Oppenheim's and Samters projects stalled as the mall project encountered legal obstacles. Efforts to revitalize the Dry would continue under the administrations of Mayor Wenzel and Mayor Jim Connors.

After a decade of decay, the Dry enjoyed a rebirth of sorts in 1992 when the restoration and transformation project finally began. Just as its future seemed to be secured, however, disaster struck on May 16, 1992, when a major fire broke out on the fourth floor. Thought to have been started by a torch cutter's errant spark, the wood frame construction of the corner building fed the flames, which destroyed the roof and sent thick black smoke billowing throughout the city. Torrents of water used to fight the fire rained down from the top floor to the basement, causing significant damage. So serious was the disaster, Wyoming Avenue had to be closed as well as all the businesses along it, including The Globe. While gobsmacked spectators watched from the entrances and windows, quick-thinking Globe staff members shut down the building's air-conditioning and circulation systems, thereby heading off a potential disaster for that store. When the flames were doused and the smoke cleared, the full scope of the devastation was revealed. The Dry's fourth floor was a smoldering ruin piled with the charred remains of the roof and interior furnishings. The other floors sustained significant smoke and water damage. While its newer concrete and steel-reinforced construction spared it the devastation that its older wood and iron sibling sustained, the Lewis & Reilly building was also heavily damaged. As serious as the fire was, however, it should be noted that it could have been far worse. Thanks to the bravery, persistence and skill of the local firefighters who

Scranton firefighters battle the blaze that engulfed the upper floors of the Oppenheim Building in May 1992. *From the Mark Boock Collection. Courtesy of Greg Boock.*

battled the flames throughout the night, one of Scranton's most treasured architectural gems was saved from complete destruction.

After the remains of the fire damage were cleared, work on the Dry continued. Like a phoenix from the ashes, the building emerged from disaster and reopened as the Oppenheim Office Center in 1993 in conjunction with the new Mall at Steamtown. Since then, the Dry has been home to several high-profile business offices, including those for AT&T, NatWest Banking, the Social Security Administration and a small newsroom for local news affiliates WYOU and WBRE. It has also housed offices for many prominent lawyers, politicians and businessmen. In 2020, it was announced that the Dry would again undergo a transformation. This time, it would become a premium apartment complex with space for offices and ground-level retail. At the time of this writing, the exterior façade has received a thorough makeover with dark bronze accents now accentuating the intricate detail of Lansing Holden's neoclassical masterpiece. Crowning the building is a rooftop bar, which gives patrons and spectators breathtaking views of the cityscape and surrounding Appalachian Mountains. Initially opening as a pop-up bar in the summer of 2024, it proved to be very popular. Decades after the store's closing, the Oppenheim Building is once again known for offering diners exciting vistas while they enjoy delicious food and drink. The legacy of the famous Tea Room lives on.

The Globe and the Dry Goods buildings, without their longtime retail tenants to sustain them, faced uncertain futures before Scranton's downtown renaissance in the 1990s. Escaping the fate of many of their brethren in other cities, both buildings have been granted a new lease on life thanks to their ability to adapt to the changing needs of the local economy. Although they are no longer the leading members of the local retail scene, they are once again indispensable parts of life in downtown Scranton.

Epilogue

PRICELESS LEGACIES

Decades have passed since Scrantonians could shop all around The Globe and never leave Scranton or park, shop and dine at their friendly department store, Oppenheim's Scranton Dry Goods Company. Nevertheless, the countless memories that were made at the two retail institutions live on in the minds and hearts of those who experienced their magic firsthand. Those memories are trickling down to generations too young to remember them thanks to the stories lovingly told to them by their elders. As Scranton looks back, it has honored the history of its great department stores in many ways.

The Globe: Still Revolving

In recent years, The Globe has enjoyed a resurgence in popularity thanks to the nostalgia generated on social media, local television and live events. Technology continues to play an important role in preserving the memory of The Globe inasmuch as it has enabled former shoppers and employees to reconnect and share their stories no matter on what part of the "globe" they currently reside. One of the best examples of this exists on Facebook, a social media website, where the group "Globe Store Scranton PA" boasts over six thousand members who regularly share stories, memories and mementos of the store. Innumerable other pages, posts and photos exist throughout the web that help keep The Globe's story alive.

In addition to social media, public television paid homage to The Globe in 2015 when local PBS affiliate WVIA produced a brief spot chronicling the store as part of its "Back in the Day" program, which was a special focusing on the history of several local institutions. Former buyer Rita Lissefeld warmly described her experiences as a staff member at The Globe while vintage photos and the store's famous television commercial were shown. One rekindled memory of the store was of its famous commercial jingle, which became an earworm to many Northeastern Pennsylvanians in the 1980s:

You can shop all around The Globe and never leave Scranton!
You can shop all around The Globe and still be close to home!
The latest fashions, your favorite styles you'll find around The Globe!
Everything you need, and so much more!
You'll find it all in just one store!
You can shop all around The Globe and never leave Scranton![263]

This documentary was well-received by viewers who were anxious to relive the memory of the store as well as that of the other establishments covered.

Those who wanted to relive The Globe in-person had the opportunity to do so in 2016 when Lackawanna County reopened the building in time for that year's holiday season. Hoping to generate excitement for its "Lackawanna Winter Market," the county sought to re-create the feeling of downtown shopping by allowing local vendors to set up shop on the largely vacant street floor. To add to the nostalgia of the event, large photos of children visiting Santa Claus during the store's glory years lined the walls while miniature train displays attracted the attention of the young and young at heart. For the first time since the mid-1990s, visitors also had the opportunity to visit Santa Claus at The Globe; St. Nick had reclaimed his throne at the old store for a brief time. To top everything off, the county re-created The Globe's beloved Christmas façade with lighted trees, swags of garland and pine wreaths. During light-up night, hundreds packed Wyoming Avenue while local choirs serenaded them with Christmas carols. So popular was the market, the county again chose the site for its 2017 and 2018 markets, the last of which moved outside due to The Globe becoming the Lackawanna County Government Center.

Over twenty years after it sold its last winter coat and prom dress, The Globe became a marketable entity in and of itself when a line of merchandise

The Lackawanna County Government Center at The Globe. *Courtesy of Cory Packer.*

featuring the store's likeness and logo was produced. Those anxious for a bit of nostalgia could purchase Christmas ornaments, pillows, mugs, candles, T-shirts, tote bags and even paintings featuring likenesses of its iconic logo and holiday façade. Although the institution itself is no more, The Globe's story has come full circle, and it is now featured on the shelves and in the windows of several other downtown stores.

The Dry: A Legacy of Giving

Although The Globe tends to receive more attention, the Dry is just as beloved to locals who remember the excitement of watching the crowds from their perch on the mezzanine or waiting in the cold for Santa and Mrs. Claus to appear on the Wyoming Avenue marquee. Like The Globe, the Dry's legacy lives on in Scranton in many ways. The most important of these is the spirit of giving demonstrated by the store and instilled in those who worked there by its founder, I.E. Oppenheim, and his descendants. This spirit endures as the Oppenheim family's

The Oppenheim Building as it appears today. *Courtesy of Cory Packer.*

contributions to faith, art, education and community continue to better the area and its residents.

Nowhere is the Dry better known and appreciated than in the hearts of those who made it hum for so many years. To celebrate their experiences, Jane and Richard Oppenheim organized a reunion of former employees in 1995. Though the building's renovated interior bore little resemblance to its retail past, retired staff could be seen laughing, conversing and remembering the place and the people that made the Dry so special.

Scranton's great department stores are gone forever. They will, however, continue to influence the soul of the city because of the indelible mark they made on time. They grew with the area, basked in its prosperity and, sadly, echoed its downfall. Their former homes found new life as the Electric City reinvented and reinvigorated itself, but it is the stores themselves that helped build it and its people. The Globe and the Dry brought the best the world had to offer and laid it at the feet of Northeastern Pennsylvanians. Their legacy of style, service and love of community will surely endure for all those who call Scranton home.

RECIPES FROM THE CHARL-MONT

Chicken Chow Mein

In a deep skillet, heat:

¼ cup cooking oil
¼ teaspoon salt
¼ teaspoon pepper

Then add:

2 cups sliced cabbage
3 cups thinly sliced celery
1 No. 303 can (approximately 2 cups) drained bean sprouts
2 teaspoons sugar

Stir and cook 10 to 15 minutes.

In 2 cups chicken stock or water, blend:

2½ tablespoons cornstarch
¼ cup cold water
¼ cup soy sauce

Add this to vegetable mixture and cook until it thickens. Then add 2 cups of sliced, cooked chicken.

Serve with chow mein noodles. Makes four to six servings.[264]

Deviled Crabmeat

1 ½ cups milk
1 ½ cups soft breadcrumbs
2 cups cooked crab meat (2 [7-oz] cans)
Whites of 5 hard-boiled eggs (mashed)
1 ½ teaspoons salt
⅓ teaspoon dry mustard
⅛ teaspoon cayenne pepper
½ cup melted butter

Combine milk and breadcrumbs, and then stir in remaining ingredients. Pour into buttered baking dish; sprinkle crumbs and butter on top. Bake 15 to 20 minutes at 450 degrees. Serves 6 to 8.[265]

Lemon Ice-Box Pie

1 can condensed milk, ice cold
3 egg yolks
Juice of 2 lemons
Graham crackers
Vanilla wafers

Blend the milk and egg yolks; add lemon juice and stir until thick. Pour into a graham cracker pie shell that is lined around the edges with vanilla wafers. Use the egg whites to whip meringue, which is spread on top of pie. Crumble a few vanilla wafers over the top and place in oven that has been preheated to 400 degrees until the top is golden brown. Cool in refrigerator and serve.[266]

Cream of Broccoli Soup

6 ounces chopped broccoli
2 cups chicken stock
4 tablespoons butter
4 tablespoons flour
4 cups of milk
½ teaspoon salt
¼ teaspoon pepper
Dash cooking sherry (optional)

Cook broccoli in chicken stock until tender. Melt butter; add flour and cook for 5 minutes. Do not brown. Add milk, broccoli and chicken stock. Stir lightly and add seasonings and wine. Yields 8 cups.

Note: Vegetables such as asparagus or carrots may be substituted for broccoli.[267]

NOTES

1. Setting Sale for New Waters

1. Beck, *Never Before in History*, 53–55.
2. Beck, *Never Before in History*, 26.
3. Beck, *Never Before in History*, 44–46, 81.
4. Beck, *Never Before in History*, 83.
5. Beck, *Never Before in History*, 83.
6. Hitchcock, *History of Scranton*, 141.
7. Hitchcock, *History of Scranton*, 141.
8. Hitchcock, *History of Scranton*, 141.
9. Hitchcock, *History of Scranton*, 141.
10. "John Cleland Dies as Result of the Second Stroke of Paralysis," *Scranton Truth*, January 6, 1912.
11. "John Cleland Dies."
12. "John Cleland Dies."
13. "John Cleland Dies."
14. "John Cleland Dies."
15. "John Cleland Dies."
16. "John Cleland Dies."
17. Hitchcock, *History of Scranton*, 141.
18. Moran-Savakinus, "Cleland Simpson Co."
19. "John Cleland Dies."

20. "Death Takes President of Globe Store," *Tribune* (Scranton, PA), December 15, 1936.
21. Moran-Savakinus, "Cleland Simpson Co."
22. Moran-Savakinus, "Cleland Simpson Co."
23. Hitchcock, *History of Scranton*, 141.
24. Kashuba, Miller-Lanning and Sweeney, *Scranton*, 64.
25. Kashuba, Miller-Lanning and Sweeney, *Scranton*, 64.
26. I Kashuba, Miller-Lanning and Sweeney, *Scranton*, 64.
27. "History of The Globe," *Globe Trotter*, June 1969.
28. Moran-Savakinus, "Cleland Simpson Co."
29. Hitchcock, *History of Scranton*, 141.
30. Hitchcock, *History of Scranton*, 141.
31. Hitchcock, *History of Scranton*, 141.
32. "Notice of Dissolution," *Tribune*, August 4, 1896.
33. "Notice of Dissolution," *Tribune*, June 8, 1901.
34. Beck, *Never Before in History*, 116.
35. The Globe Warehouse advertisement, *Tribune-Republican*, February 15, 1913.
36. Beck, *Never Before in History*, 116.
37. Beck, *Never Before in History*, 116.
38. "John Cleland Dies."
39. "Last Rites Scheduled for I.E. Oppenheim," *Scranton Times*, February 22, 1954.
40. Keith Oppenheim, correspondence with the author, March 17, 2022.
41. Oppenheim, correspondence.
42. Oppenheim, correspondence.
43. Oppenheim, correspondence.
44. Oppenheim, correspondence.
45. "Growth of Akron Dry Goods Co. Is Credit to Owners," *Akron Beacon Journal*, July 21, 1925.
46. "Growth of Akron Dry Goods Co."
47. "Growth of Akron Dry Goods Co."
48. "Growth of Akron Dry Goods Co."
49. "Lehman Brothers Advertisement," *Brooklyn Daily Times*, February 20, 1928.
50. "Lehman Brothers Advertisement."
51. "Growth of Akron Dry Goods Co."
52. "Growth of Akron Dry Goods Co."
53. "Growth of Akron Dry Goods Co."

54. "Growth of Akron Dry Goods Co."
55. "Growth of Akron Dry Goods Co."
56. "Growth of Akron Dry Goods Co."
57. "Growth of Akron Dry Goods Co."
58. "Growth of Akron Dry Goods Co."
59. "Metropolitan Home of Scranton Dry Goods Co. Will Open Its Doors to the Public Tomorrow," *Scranton Truth*, March 8, 1912.
60. "M.J. Federman to Locate Here," *Scranton Truth*, January 3, 1912.
61. "M.J. Federman to Locate Here."
62. "Metropolitan Home of Scranton Dry Goods Co."
63. "Metropolitan Home of Scranton Dry Goods Co."
64. "Metropolitan Home of Scranton Dry Goods Co."
65. "Metropolitan Home of Scranton Dry Goods Co."
66. "Metropolitan Home of Scranton Dry Goods Co."
67. "Metropolitan Home of Scranton Dry Goods Co."
68. "I.E. Oppenheim and Constance Mendel Marriage Announcement," *Indianapolis News*, December 22, 1909.

2. Escalating Success

69. "The Globe in Ruins," *Scranton Republican*, April 3, 1889.
70. "Globe in Ruins."
71. "Contractor Williams Had General Contact for Remodeling Globe Store," *Scranton Times*, September 14, 1917.
72. "Sanitary Plumbing at New Globe Store by Wolf & Wenzel," *Scranton Times*, September 14, 1917.
73. "Schillinger Brothers Doing Bulk of Work Hereabouts," *Scranton Times*, September 14, 1917.
74. "Schillinger Brothers Doing Bulk of Work Hereabouts."
75. "Schillinger Brothers Doing Bulk of Work Hereabouts."
76. "Today, The Globe Store Is Really 35.8 Miles Long," *Tribune*, September 26, 1953.
77. "Today, The Globe Store."
78. "Today, The Globe Store."
79. "The Globe 70th Anniversary Sale," *Tribune*, October 11, 1948.
80. "Globe Store Officials Prepare for New Men's Shop Opening," *Scrantonian*, September 12, 1948.

81. "Globe Store Officials Prepare."
82. "Globe Store Officials Prepare."
83. "Globe Store Officials Prepare."
84. "Globe Store Officials Prepare."
85. "Vineberg Is Now Owner of Akron Dry Goods Store," *Akron Beacon Journal*, November 27, 1927.
86. Thackara, "Oppenheim's Opened as Business in 1912."
87. "Col. Long Says Big Stores Will Seek New Site; Oppenheim Buys Property for $600,000," *Scranton Times*, August 8, 1916.
88. "Col. Long Says Big Stores Will Seek New Site."
89. "Col. Long Says Big Stores Will Seek New Site."
90. Hendrickson, *Grand Emporiums*, 446.
91. "Col. Long Says Big Stores Will Seek New Site."
92. "Col. Long Says Big Stores Will Seek New Site."
93. "Wrap Girl's Memory," *Scranton Times*, December 10, 1980.
94. "Wrap Girl's Memory."
95. "Wrap Girl's Memory."
96. "Wrap Girl's Memory."
97. "Wrap Girl's Memory."
98. "Wrap Girl's Memory."
99. "Wrap Girl's Memory."
100. Kashuba, Miller-Lanning and Sweeney, *Scranton*, 26.
101. "Long's Sons' New Store," *Wilkes-Barre Times*, May 31, 1897.
102. "Long's Sons' New Store."
103. "Col. Long Says Big Stores Will Seek New Site."
104. "Col. Long Says Big Stores Will Seek New Site."
105. "Col. Long Says Big Stores Will Seek New Site."
106. "Col. Long Says Big Stores Will Seek New Site."
107. "Col. Long Says Big Stores Will Seek New Site."
108. "Col. Long Says Big Stores Will Seek New Site."
109. "Col. Long Says Big Stores Will Seek New Site."
110. "Col. Long Says Big Stores Will Seek New Site."
111. "Globe Store Takes Over the Stock of Jonas Long's Sons," *Scranton Times*, January 9, 1917.
112. "Globe Store Takes Over the Stock."
113. "Col. Long Says Big Stores Will Seek New Site."
114. "Col. Long Says Big Stores Will Seek New Site."
115. "Master Architect Designed Big Store," *Scranton Republican*, July 18, 1917.

116. "Gas Company a Factor in City Development," *Scranton Republican*, July 18, 1917.
117. "Opening of Giant Store Marks Epoch," *Scranton Republican*, July 18, 1917.
118. "Opening of Giant Store."
119. "Opening of Giant Store."
120. "Opening of Giant Store."
121. Hitchcock, *History of Scranton*, 151–52.
122. Hitchcock, *History of Scranton*, 151–52.
123. Hitchcock, *History of Scranton*, 151–52.
124. Hitchcock, *History of Scranton*, 151–52.
125. Hitchcock, *History of Scranton*, 151–52.
126. Hitchcock, *History of Scranton*, 151–52.
127. Hitchcock, *History of Scranton*, 151–52.
128. Hitchcock, *History of Scranton*, 151–52.
129. Hitchcock, *History of Scranton*, 151–52.
130. Hitchcock, *History of Scranton*, 151–52.
131. "Scranton Dry Goods Company's New Home as It Will Look When Addition Now in Progress of Construction Is Completed," *Scranton Times*, May 26, 1925.
132. "Scranton Dry Goods Company's New Home."
133. "Scranton Store Expands for Fourth Time in Fourteen Years," *Dry Goods Economist*, June 5, 1926.
134. "Scranton Store Expands."
135. "Scranton Store Expands."
136. "Scranton Store Expands."
137. "Scranton Store Expands."
138. "Scranton Store Expands."
139. "Scranton Store Expands."
140. "Scranton Store Expands."
141. "Scranton Store Expands."
142. "Scranton Store Expands."
143. "Scranton Store Expands."
144. "Scranton Store Expands."
145. "Scranton Store Expands."
146. "Scranton Store Expands."
147. Scranton Dry Goods Company advertisement, *Scranton Republican*, October 4, 1924.
148. Scranton Dry Goods Company advertisement.

149. "Kiddies Enjoy Ride on City's First Escalators," *Scranton Republican*, October 8, 1924.
150. Addie Warenzak, in discussion with the author, May 10, 2018.
151. Warenzak, discussion.
152. "Scranton Store Expands."
153. "Scranton Store Expands."
154. "Last Rites."
155. "Last Rites."
156. John M. Hart Jr., "Oppenheim's Closes Doors After 68 Years in Business," *Scrantonian*, November 2, 1980.
157. Thackara, "Oppenheim's Opened."
158. Hart, "Oppenheim's Closes."
159. "Scranton Dry Goods Will Keep Up with City Growth: Oppenheim," *Scranton Times*, February 26, 1962.
160. "Scranton Dry Goods Will Keep Up."
161. Coveleskie, "Oppenheim's Rebirth Stirs Memories of Glory Days."

3. Parking Space

162. "Restaurant in Globe Annex to Seat 250," *Scranton Tribune*, August 21, 1957.
163. "Publication Honors City Architect for Designs of Store Expansion," *Scranton Tribune*, January 21, 1956.
164. Scranton Dry Goods Company Car Park advertisement, *Century Club Bulletin*, October 1959.
165. Warenzak, discussion.

4. The Finest in Cuisine…The Most Excellent in Service… The Ultimate in Dining

166. Charl-Mont Restaurant advertisement, *Scrantonian*, October 17, 1976.
167. Charl-Mont Restaurant advertisement.
168. Bensing, "Chef's Corner."
169. Lisicky, "Charl Was Charles Price."
170. Spuds Restaurant advertisement, *Tribune*, March 12, 1980.

171. "Scranton Store Expands."
172. Scranton Dry Goods Company Tea Room Menu, 1937.
173. Brislin, "Drifting 'n' Dining."
174. Antoinette Altieri, in discussion with the author, 2004.
175. Brislin, "Drifiting 'n' Dining."
176. Scranton Dry Goods Company Tea Room Menu, 1964.

5. Holiday Headquarters

177. Warenzak, discussion.
178. Rita Lissefeld, interview by Larry Vojtko, *Back in the Day*, VIA Studios Global, 2014, video, 26:23.
179. "It's Beginning to Look a Lot Like Christmas All Around The Globe," *Globe Trotter*, November 1969.
180. DeAndrea, "They Spice the Season."
181. DeAndrea, "They Spice the Season."
182. DeAndrea, "They Spice the Season."
183. Bonifanti, "Doll Hospital Reopens."

6. The Ten Commandments of Good Business

184. Makarevich, "Lower Air Conditioning Edict."
185. "Appearance," *Globe Trotter*, April 1972.
186. "Ten Commandments of Good Business," *Globe Trotter*, June 1974.
187. Hess, *Every Dollar Counts*, 43–46.
188. "New Escalator Begins Function at Dry Goods," *Scranton Tribune*, October 11, 1968.
189. Coveleskie, "Oppenheim's Rebirth."

7. Fashion Floor

190. Hess, *Every Dollar Counts*, 70.
191. Hess, *Every Dollar Counts*, 71.
192. Hess, *Every Dollar Counts*, 72–73.

193. Hess, *Every Dollar Counts*, 73.
194. Ellis Oppenheim Jr. correspondence.
195. Ellis Oppenheim Jr. correspondence.

8. A Tree Grows in Scranton

196. "Girl Scout Cookie Day in Store," *Globe Trotter*, March 1971.
197. "Diabetes Tests Conducted," *Globe Trotter*, May 1970.
198. "Association for Blind Lists Helen Keller Day," *Scranton Tribune*, November 16, 1970.
199. "Scranton Dry Gives Elevator to City Schools," *Scranton Times*, April 10, 1958.
200. "Last Rites."
201. "Ellis Oppenheim Dies," *Tribune*, December 7, 1983.
202. "Former Dry Goods Merchant Richard E. Oppenheim Dies," *Scranton Times*, November 24, 1995.
203. "Jane Ellenbogen Oppenheim," *Scranton Times*, June 12, 2021.
204. "Scranton Dry Goods Gets National Award," *Scranton Times*, August 12, 1971.

9. Growing Branches

205. Lisicky, *Shop Pomeroy's First*, 74.
206. Lisicky, *Shop Pomeroy's First*, 74–75.
207. "New Facility Demonstrates Globe Store's Faith in Area," *Sunday Times*, April 7, 1968.
208. Lisicky, *Wanamaker's*, 99.
209. Lisicky, *Wanamaker's*, 99.
210. Lisicky, *Wanamaker's*, 20.
211. Lisicky, *Wanamaker's*, 21.
212. Lisicky, *Wanamaker's*, 22–23.
213. Lisicky, *Wanamaker's*, 28.
214. Lisicky, *Wanamaker's*, 32.
215. Lisicky, *Wanamaker's*, 34
216. Lisicky, *Wanamaker's*, 21.

217. "Scranton Dry Will Open Summit 'Country Store,'" *Scranton Tribune*, March 19, 1965.
218. "Oppenheim's to Open Store in Pocono Mall," *Scranton Tribune*, June 12, 1973.

10. Going Down

219. Lisicky, *Wanamaker's*, 121.
220. "Scranton Dry Goods Retitled Oppenheim's," *Scranton Tribune*, February 28, 1972.

11. The Ladies Vanish

221. "Preston Named as Globe's Chief Executive," *Scranton Times*, February 28, 1979.
222. Beck, *Never Before in History*, 117.
223. "Preston Named as Globe's Chief Executive."
224. Lisicky, *Wanamaker's*, 111.
225. Lisicky, *Wanamaker's*, 111.
226. Lisicky, *Wanamaker's*, 111.
227. Lisicky, *Wanamaker's*, 114
228. Lisicky, *Wanamaker's*, 112.
229. Lisicky, *Wanamaker's*, 120.
230. Lisicky, *Wanamaker's*, 120.
231. Lisicky, *Wanamaker's*, 120.
232. Lisicky, *Wanamaker's*, 120.
233. The Globe advertisement, *Scranton Times*, August 3, 1988.
234. Coveleskie, "Globe Among Top Stores in U.S."
235. "Preston Departs from Globe Store," *Scranton Times*, June 28, 1991.
236. Coveleskie, "New Globe Store Owner."
237. Haggerty, "Globe's Loyal Customers."
238. Haggerty, "Globe's Loyal Customers."
239. Bogino, "Some Creditors Left Out."
240. Bogino, "Some Creditors Left Out."

241. Bogino, "Some Creditors Left Out."
242. Singleton, "Judge Oks Liquidation."
243. Bogino, "Some Creditors Left Out."
244. Obrzut, "Spanning the Globe."
245. Obrzut, "Spanning the Globe."
246. Obrzut, "Spanning the Globe."
247. "The End of an Era," Boscov's advertisement, *Scranton Times*, February 18, 1994.
248. "Oppenheim's Staying Open," *Tribune*, January 4, 1979/
249. "Meeting Called for Feb. 4 to Discuss Decline of Downtown Business District," *Scranton Times*, January 19, 1977.
250. "Officials Optimistic About Oppenheim's," *Tribune*, January 19, 1979.
251. "Oppenheim's Offers Plan of Payments," *Scranton Times*, July 9, 1979.
252. "Oppenheim's Offers Plan of Payments."
253. "Oppenheim's Staying Open."
254. "Oppenheim's Staying Open."
255. Coleman, "Era Bows Out in Shock."
256. Coleman, "Era Bows Out in Shock."
257. Coleman, "Era Bows Out in Shock."
258. Flannery, "Scranton Dry."

12. Grand Reopening

259. Ackerman, with Marriggi, *I Have an Idea*, 162.
260. Ackerman, with Marriggi, *I Have an Idea*, 162–63.
261. Ackerman, with Marriggi, *I Have an Idea*, 163.
262. Katz, "Holmes Is Bringing a Bit."

Epilogue

263. Rita Lissefeld, interview, 19:29-19:58.

Recipes from the Charl-Mont

264. Bensing, "Chef's Corner."
265. Bensing, "Chef's Corner."
266. Bensing, "Chef's Corner."
267. Conrad, "Cream Soup from the Charl-Mont."

BIBLIOGRAPHY

Ackerman, Ed, with Marlene Marriggi. *I Have an Idea*. Independent Graphics, 2021.

Akron Beacon Journal. "Growth of Akron Dry Goods Co. Is Credit to Owners." July 21, 1925.

———. "Vineberg Is Now Owner of Akron Dry Goods Store." November 27, 1927.

Beck, John. *Never Before in History: The Story of Scranton*. Windsor Publications, 1986.

Bensing, Gus. "Chef's Corner." *Times-Tribune*, August 8, 1960.

Bogino, Charles H. "Some Creditors Left Out as Judge OKs Globe Sale." *The Times-Leader*, February 16, 1994.

Bonifanti, Terry. "Doll Hospital Reopens Despite Store's Closing." *The Scranton Times*, December 5, 1980.

Brislin, Gene. "Drifting 'n' Dining." *The Scranton Tribune*, January 14, 1977.

Brooklyn Daily Times. "Lehman Brothers Advertisement." February 20, 1928.

Century Club Bulletin. Scranton Dry Goods Company Car Park Advertisement. October 1959. https://digitalarchives.powerlibrary.org.

Coleman, Gene. "Era Bows Out in Shock and Tears as 'Scranton Dry' Closes Its Doors." *The Sunday Times*, November 2, 1980.

Conrad, Lenny. "Cream Soup from the Charl-Mont." *The Times-Tribune*, May 8, 1983.

Coveleskie, Vince. "The Globe Among Top Stores in U.S." *The Scranton Times*, December 25, 1987.

———. "New Globe Store Owner Making Major Changes." *The Scranton Times*, September 15, 1991.

———. "Oppenheim's Rebirth Stirs Memories of Glory Days." *The Scranton Times*, September 12, 1993.

DeAndrea, Frances T. "They Spice the Season with Window-Dressing." *The Scranton Times*, November 26, 1977.

Dry Goods Economist. "Scranton Store Expands for Fourth Time in Fourteen Years." June 5, 1926.

Flannery, Joseph X. "Scranton Dry: Treasure House of Memories." *The Scranton Times*, December 4, 1980.

The Globe Trotter. "Appearance." April 1972.

———. "Diabetes Tests Conducted." May 1970.

———. "Girl Scout Cookie Day in Store." March 1971.

———. "History of The Globe." June 1969.

———. "It's Beginning to Look a Lot Like Christmas All Around the Globe." November 1969.

———. "The Ten Commandments of Good Business." June 1974.

Haggerty, Mauri. "The Globe's Loyal Customers Feel Like They've Lost a Friend." *The Scranton Times*, February 10, 1994.

Hart, John M., Jr. "Oppenheim's Closes Doors After 68 Years in Business." *The Scrantonian*, November 2, 1980.

Hendrickson, Robert. *The Grand Emporiums: The Illustrated History of America's Great Department Stores*. Stein and Day/Scarborough House, 1979.

Hess, Max, Jr. *Every Dollar Counts*. New York Fairchild Publications Inc., 1952.

Hitchcock, Frederick Lyman. *History of Scranton and Its People*. Vol. 2. Lewis Historical Publishing Company, 1914.

The Indianapolis News. "I.E. Oppenheim and Constance Mendel Marriage Announcement." December 22, 1909.

Kashuba, Cheryl A., Darlene Miller-Lanning and Alan Sweeney. *Scranton*. Arcadia Publishing, 2005.

Katz, Michael. "Holmes Is Bringing a Bit of Glory Back to Scranton." *New York Times*, March 27, 1983.

Lisicky, Michael J. "The Charl Was Charles Price…" Facebook, May 3, 2018, https://m.facebook.com.

———. *Shop Pomeroy's First*. The History Press, 2014.

———. *Wanamaker's: Meet Me at the Eagle*. The History Press, 2010.

Lissefeld, Rita. Interview by Larry Vojtko. *Back in the Day*, VIA Studios Global, 2014. Video, 26:23.

Makarevich, Jerry. "Lower Air Conditioning Edict Produces Shopper Complaints." *The Scranton Times*, July 24, 1979.

Moran-Savakinus, Mary Ann. "Cleland Simpson Co.—A Short History of the Globe Store." *Active Senior*. January 2000.

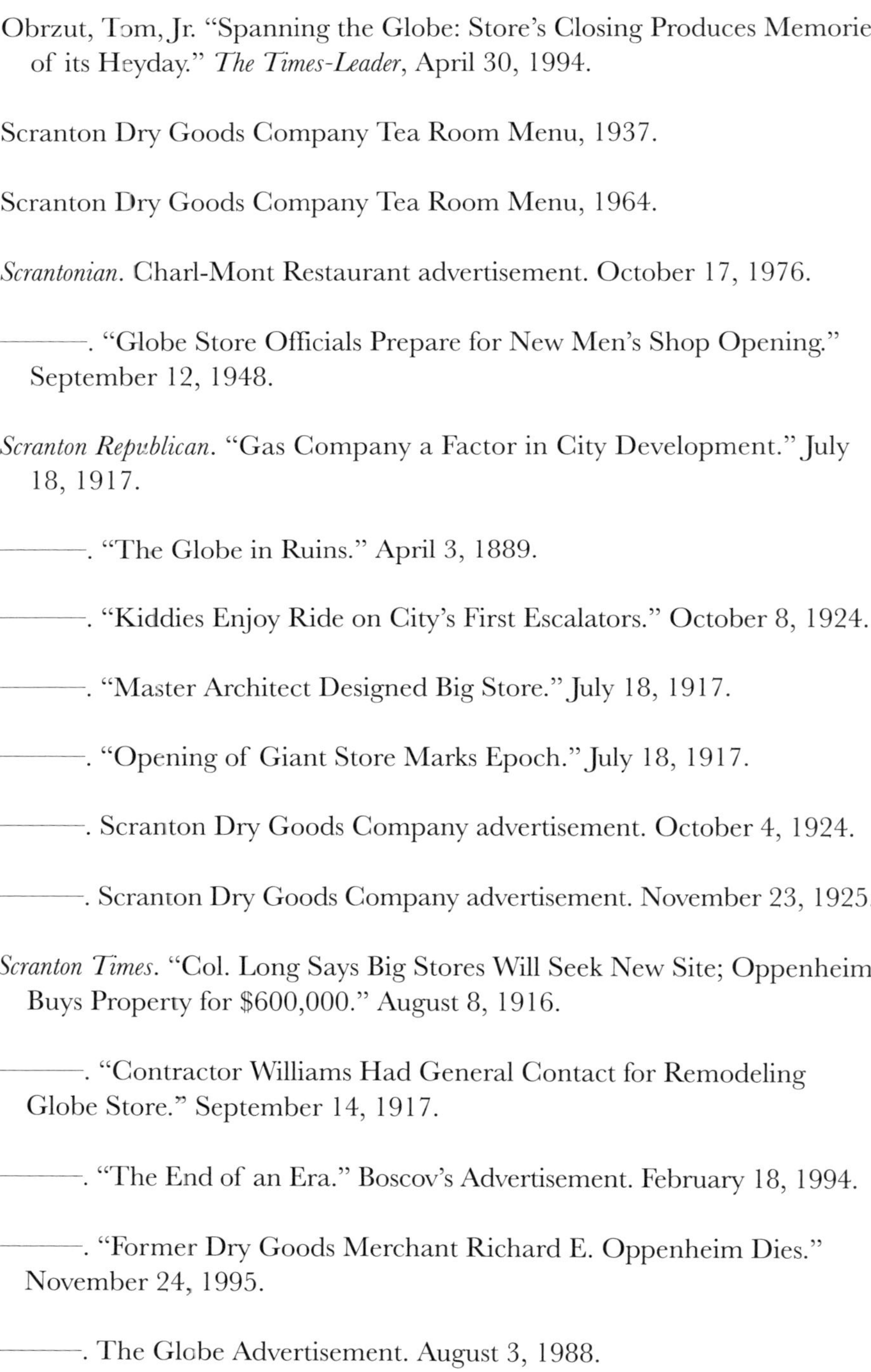

Obrzut, Tom, Jr. "Spanning the Globe: Store's Closing Produces Memories of its Heyday." *The Times-Leader*, April 30, 1994.

Scranton Dry Goods Company Tea Room Menu, 1937.

Scranton Dry Goods Company Tea Room Menu, 1964.

Scrantonian. Charl-Mont Restaurant advertisement. October 17, 1976.

———. "Globe Store Officials Prepare for New Men's Shop Opening." September 12, 1948.

Scranton Republican. "Gas Company a Factor in City Development." July 18, 1917.

———. "The Globe in Ruins." April 3, 1889.

———. "Kiddies Enjoy Ride on City's First Escalators." October 8, 1924.

———. "Master Architect Designed Big Store." July 18, 1917.

———. "Opening of Giant Store Marks Epoch." July 18, 1917.

———. Scranton Dry Goods Company advertisement. October 4, 1924.

———. Scranton Dry Goods Company advertisement. November 23, 1925.

Scranton Times. "Col. Long Says Big Stores Will Seek New Site; Oppenheim Buys Property for $600,000." August 8, 1916.

———. "Contractor Williams Had General Contact for Remodeling Globe Store." September 14, 1917.

———. "The End of an Era." Boscov's Advertisement. February 18, 1994.

———. "Former Dry Goods Merchant Richard E. Oppenheim Dies." November 24, 1995.

———. The Globe Advertisement. August 3, 1988.

———. "Globe Store Takes Over the Stock of Jonas Long's Sons." January 9, 1917.

———. "Last Rites Scheduled for I.E. Oppenheim." February 22, 1954.

———. "Meeting Called for Feb. 4 to Discuss Decline of Downtown Business District." January 19, 1977.

———. "Oppenheim's Offers Plan of Payments." July 9, 1979.

———. "Preston Departs from Globe Store." June 28, 1991.

———. "Preston Named as Globe's Chief Executive." February 28, 1979.

———. "Sanitary Plumbing at New Globe Store by Wolf & Wenzel." September 14, 1917.

———. "Schillinger Brothers Doing Bulk of Work Hereabouts." September 14, 1917.

———. "Scranton Dry Gives Elevator to City Schools." April 10, 1958.

———. "Scranton Dry Goods Company's New Home as It Will Look When Addition Now in Progress of Construction Is Completed." May 26, 1925.

———. "Scranton Dry Goods Gets National Award." August 12, 1971.

———. "Scranton Dry Goods Will Keep Up with City Growth: Oppenheim." February 26, 1962.

———. "Wrap Girl's Memory." December 10, 1980.

Scranton Tribune. "Association for Blind Lists Helen Keller Day." November 16, 1970.

———. "Oppenheim's to Open Store in Pocono Mall." June 12, 1973.

———. "Publication Honors City Architect for Designs of Store Expansion." January 21, 1956.

———. "Restaurant in Globe Annex to Seat 250." August 21, 1957.

———. "Scranton Dry Goods Retitled Oppenheim's." February 28, 1972.

———. "Scranton Dry Will Open Summit 'Country Store.'" March 19, 1965.

Scranton Truth. "John Cleland Dies as Result of the Second Stroke of Paralysis." January 6, 1912.

———. "Metropolitan Home of Scranton Dry Goods Co. Will Open Its Doors to the Public Tomorrow." March 8, 1912.

———. "M.J. Federman to Locate Here." January 3, 1912.

Singleton, David. "Judge Oks Liquidation of Globe Inventory." *The Tribune*. February 16, 1994.

Sunday Times. "New Facility Demonstrates Globe Store's Faith in Area." April 7, 1968.

Thackara, Gina. "Oppenheim's Opened as Business in 1912." *The Scranton Times*, undated clipping.

Tribune. "Death Takes President of Globe Store." December 15, 1936.

———. "Ellis Oppenheim Dies." December 7, 1983.

———. "The Globe 70th Anniversary Sale." October 11, 1948.

———. "Notice of Dissolution." August 4, 1896.

———. "Notice of Dissolution." June 8, 1901.

———. "Officials Optimistic About Oppenheim's." January 19, 1979.

———. "Oppenheim's Staying Open." January 4, 1979.

———. Spuds Restaurant advertisement. March 12, 1980.

———. "Today, The Globe Store Is Really 35.8 Miles Long." September 26, 1953.

The Tribune-Republican. The Globe Warehouse advertisement. February 15, 1913.

Wilkes-Barre Times. "Long's Sons' New Store." May 31, 1897.

ABOUT THE AUTHOR

Daniel J. Packer Jr. is a fifth-generation Northeastern Pennsylvania resident who has had a lifelong passion for researching the history of local retail, especially that of the major department stores that once graced the area's downtowns. One of his favorite hobbies is collecting memorabilia from local department stores, including The Globe Store, Oppenheim's Scranton Dry Goods Company and Hess's. His interest in local history was sparked in him by his great-grandmother Antoinette, who would spend many summer hours with her grandchildren and great-grandchildren sitting on her front porch glider. There, she recounted fascinating tales of her childhood and young adulthood spent in the Electric City and the surrounding countryside during the first half of the twentieth century. Daniel considers her to be his greatest history teacher. Today, he endeavors to carry on her legacy by preserving and recounting historical stories of local interest to future generations.